Don Sebastian by John Dryden

A TRAGEDY.

—Nec tarda senectus
Debilitat vires animi, mutatque vigorem.
VIRG.

John Dryden was born on August 9th, 1631 in the village rectory of Aldwincle near Thrapston in Northamptonshire. As a boy Dryden lived in the nearby village of Titchmarsh, Northamptonshire. In 1644 he was sent to Westminster School as a King's Scholar.

Dryden obtained his BA in 1654, graduating top of the list for Trinity College, Cambridge that year.

Returning to London during The Protectorate, Dryden now obtained work with Cromwell's Secretary of State, John Thurloe.

At Cromwell's funeral on 23 November 1658 Dryden was in the company of the Puritan poets John Milton and Andrew Marvell. The setting was to be a sea change in English history. From Republic to Monarchy and from one set of lauded poets to what would soon become the Age of Dryden.

The start began later that year when Dryden published the first of his great poems, Heroic Stanzas (1658), a eulogy on Cromwell's death.

With the Restoration of the Monarchy in 1660 Dryden celebrated in verse with Astraea Redux, an authentic royalist panegyric.

With the re-opening of the theatres after the Puritan ban, Dryden began to also write plays. His first play, The Wild Gallant, appeared in 1663 but was not successful. From 1668 on he was contracted to produce three plays a year for the King's Company, in which he became a shareholder. During the 1660s and '70s, theatrical writing was his main source of income.

In 1667, he published Annus Mirabilis, a lengthy historical poem which described the English defeat of the Dutch naval fleet and the Great Fire of London in 1666. It established him as the pre-eminent poet of his generation, and was crucial in his attaining the posts of Poet Laureate (1668) and then historiographer royal (1670).

This was truly the Age of Dryden, he was the foremost English Literary figure in Poetry, Plays, translations and other forms.

In 1694 he began work on what would be his most ambitious and defining work as translator, The Works of Virgil (1697), which was published by subscription. It was a national event.

John Dryden died on May 12th, 1700, and was initially buried in St. Anne's cemetery in Soho, before being exhumed and reburied in Westminster Abbey ten days later.

Index of Contents
DON SEBASTIAN. AN INTRODUCTION
TO THE RIGHT HONOURABLE PHILIP, EARL OF LEICESTER, &c.
THE PREFACE
PROLOGUE—SENT TO THE AUTHOR BY AN UNKNOWN HAND, AND PROPOSED TO BE SPOKEN BY MRS MOUNTFORD, DRESSED LIKE AN OFFICER
PROLOGUE, SPOKEN BY A WOMAN
DRAMATIS PERSONÆ
SCENE—In the Castle of Alcazar
DON SEBASTIAN, KING OF PORTUGAL.
ACT I
SCENE I
ACT II
SCENE I—Supposed to be a Terrace Walk, on the Side of the Castle of Alcazar
SCENE II—Supposed a Garden, with Lodging Rooms Behind it, or on the Sides
ACT III
SCENE I—A Terrace Walk; or some other public place in the castle of Alcazar
SCENE II.—A Night-Scene of the Mufti's Garden, Where an Arbour is Discovered
ACT IV
SCENE I.—Benducar's Palace, in the Castle of Alcazar
SCENE II.—A Night-Scene of the Mufti's Garden
SCENE III—Changes to the Castle Yard
ACT V
SCENE I—The Scene is a Room of State
EPILOGUE, SPOKEN BETWIXT ANTONIO AND MORAYMA
John Dryden – A Short Biography
John Dryden – A Concise Bibliography

DON SEBASTIAN. AN INTRODUCTION

The following tragedy is founded upon the adventures supposed to have befallen Sebastian, king of Portugal, after the fatal battle of Alcazar. The reader may be briefly reminded of the memorable expedition of that gallant monarch to Africa, to signalize, against the Moors, his chivalry as a warrior, and his faith as a Christian. The ostensible pretext of invasion was the cause of Muly Mahomet, son of Abdalla, emperor of Morocco; upon whose death, his brother, Muly Moluch, had seized the crown, and driven his nephew into exile. The armies joined battle near Alcazar. The Portuguese, far inferior in number to the Moors, displayed the most desperate valour, and had nearly won the day, when Muly Moluch, who, though almost dying, was present on the field in a litter, fired with shame and indignation, threw himself on horseback, rallied his troops, renewed the combat, and, being carried back to his litter, immediately expired, with his finger placed on his lips, to impress on the chiefs, who surrounded him, the necessity of concealing his death. The Moors, rallied by their sovereign's dying exertion, surrounded, and totally routed, the army of Sebastian. Mahomet, the competitor for the throne of Morocco, was drowned in passing a river in his flight, and Sebastian, as his body was never found, probably perished in the same manner. But where the region of historical certainty ends, that of romantic tradition commences. The Portuguese, to whom the memory of their warlike sovereign was deservedly dear, grasped at the feeble hope which the uncertainty of his fate afforded, and long, with vain fondness, expected the return of Sebastian, to free them from the yoke of Spain. This mysterious termination of a hero's career, as it gave rise to various political intrigues, (for several persons assumed the name and character of Sebastian,) early afforded a subject for exercising the fancy of the dramatist and romance writer. "The Battle of Alcazar[1]" is known to the collectors of old plays; a ballad on the same subject is reprinted in Evans's collection; and our author mentions a French novel on the adventures of Don Sebastian, to which Langbaine also refers.

The situation of Dryden, after the Revolution, was so delicate as to require great caution and attention, both in his choice of a subject, and his mode of treating it. His distressed circumstances and lessened income compelled him to come before the public as an author; while the odium attached to the proselyte of a hated religion, and the partizan of a depressed faction, was likely, upon the slightest pretext, to transfer itself from the person of the poet to the labours on which his support depended. He was, therefore, not only obliged to chuse a theme, which had no offence in it, and to treat it in a manner which could not admit of misconstruction, but also so to exert the full force of his talents, and by the conspicuous pre-eminence of his genius, to bribe prejudice and silence calumny. An observing reader will accordingly discover, throughout the following tragedy, symptoms of minute finishing, and marks of accurate attention, which, in our author's better days, he deigned not to bestow upon productions, to which his name alone was then sufficient to give weight and privilege. His choice of a subject was singularly happy: the name of Sebastian awaked historical recollections and associations, favourable to the character of his hero; while the dark uncertainty of his fate removed all possibility of shocking the audience by glaring offence against the majesty of historical truth. The subject has, therefore, all the advantages of a historical play, without the detects, which either a rigid coincidence with history, or a violent contradiction of known truth, seldom fail to bring along with them. Dryden appears from his preface to have been fully sensible of this; and he has not lost the advantage of a happy subject by treating it with the carelessness he sometimes allowed himself to indulge.

The characters in "Don Sebastian" are contrasted with singular ability and judgment. Sebastian, high-spirited and fiery; the soul of royal and military honour; the soldier and the king; almost embodies the idea which the reader forms at the first mention of his name. Dorax, to whom he is so admirable a contrast, is one of those characters whom the strong hand of adversity has wrested from their natural bias; and perhaps no equally vivid picture can be found, of a subject so awfully interesting. Born with a strong tendency to all that was honourable and virtuous, the very excess of his virtues became vice, when his own ill fate, and Sebastian's injustice, had driven him into exile. By comparing, as Dryden has requested, the character of Dorax, in the fifth act, with that he maintains in the former part of the play, the difference may be traced betwixt his natural virtues, and the vices engrafted on them by headlong passion and embittering calamity. There is no inconsistence in the change which takes place after his scene with Sebastian; as was objected by those, whom the poet justly terms, "the more ignorant sort of creatures." It is the same picture in a new light; the same ocean in tempest and in calm; the same traveller, whom sunshine has induced to abandon his cloak, which the storm only forced him to wrap more closely around him. The principal failing of Dorax is the excess of pride, which renders each supposed wound to his honour more venomously acute; yet he is not devoid of gentler affections, though even in indulging these the hardness of his character is conspicuous. He loves Violante, but that is a far subordinate feeling to his affection for Sebastian. Indeed, his love appears so inferior to his loyal devotion to his king, that, unless to gratify the taste of the age, I see little reason for its being introduced at all. It is obvious he was much more jealous of the regard of his sovereign, than of his mistress; he never mentions Violante till the scene of explanation with Sebastian; and he appears hardly to have retained a more painful recollection of his disappointment in that particular, than of the general neglect and disgrace he had sustained at the court of Lisbon. The last stage of a virtuous heart, corroded into evil by wounded pride, has been never more forcibly displayed than in the character of Dorax. When once induced to take the fatal step which degraded him in his own eyes, all his good affections seem to be converted into poison. The religion, which displays itself in the fifth act in his arguments against suicide, had, in his efforts to justify his apostacy, or at least to render it a matter of no moment, been exchanged for sentiments approaching, perhaps to atheism, certainly to total scepticism. His passion for Violante is changed into contempt and hatred for her sex, which he expresses in the coarsest terms. His feelings of generosity, and even of humanity, are drowned in the gloomy and stern misanthropy, which has its source in the self-discontent that endeavours to wreak itself upon others. This may be illustrated by his unfeeling behaviour, while Alvarez and Antonio, well known to him in former days, approach, and draw the deadly lot, which ratifies their fate. No yielding of compassion, no recollection of former friendship, has power to alter the cold and sardonic sarcasm with which he sketches their characters, and marks their deportment in that awful moment. Finally, the zealous attachment of Alonzo for his king, which, in its original expression, partakes of absolute devotion, is changed, by the circumstances of Dorax, into an irritated and frantic jealousy, which he mistakes for hatred; and which, in pursuing the destruction of its object, is almost more inveterate than hatred itself. Nothing has survived of the original Alonzo at the opening of the piece, except the gigantic passion which has caused his ruin. This character is drawn on a large scale, and in a heroic proportion; but it is so true to nature, that many readers must have lamented, even within the circle of domestic acquaintance, instances of feelings hardened, and virtues perverted, where a high spirit has sustained severe and unjust neglect and disgrace. The whole demeanour of this exquisite character suits the original sketch. From "the long stride and sullen port," by which Benducar distinguishes him at a distance, to the sullen stubbornness with which he obeys, or the haughty contempt with which he resists, the commands of the peremptory tyrant under whom he had taken service, all announce the untamed pride which had robbed Dorax of virtue, and which yet, when Benducar would seduce him into a conspiracy, and in his conduct towards Sebastian, assumes the port and dignity of virtue herself. In all his conduct and bearing, there is that mixed feeling and impulse, which constitutes the real spring of human action. The true motive of Alonzo in saving Sebastian, is not purely that of honourable hatred, which he proposes to himself; for to himself every man endeavours to appear consistent, and readily find arguments to prove to himself that he is so. Neither is his conduct to be ascribed altogether to the gentler feelings of loyal and friendly affection, relenting at the sight of his sovereign's ruin, and impending death. It is the result of a mixture of these opposite sensations, clashing against each other like two rivers at their conflux, yet urging their united course down the same channel. Actuated by a mixture of these feelings, Dorax meets Sebastian; and the art of the poet is displayed in that admirable scene, by suggesting a natural motive to justify to the injured subject himself the change of the course of his feelings. As his jealousy of Sebastian's favour, and resentment of his unjust neglect, was chiefly founded on the avowed preference which the king had given to Henriquez, the opportune mention of his rival's death, by removing the cause of that jealousy, gives the renegade an apology to his own pride, for throwing himself at the feet of that very sovereign, whom a moment before he was determined to force to combat. They are little acquainted with human passions, at least have only witnessed their operations among men of common minds, who doubt, that at the height of their very spring-tide, they are often most susceptible of sudden changes; revolutions, which seem to those who have not remarked how nearly the most opposite feelings are allied and united, the most extravagant and unaccountable. Muly Moluch is an admirable specimen of that very frequent theatrical character,—a stage tyrant. He is fierce and boisterous enough to be sufficiently terrible and odious, and that without much rant, considering he is an infidel Soldan, who, from the ancient deportment of Mahomed and Termagaunt, as they appeared in the old Mysteries, might claim a prescriptive right to tear a passion to tatters. Besides, the Moorish emperor has fine glances of savage generosity, and that free, unconstrained, and almost noble openness, the only good quality, perhaps, which a consciousness of unbounded power may encourage in a mind so firm as not to be totally depraved by it. The character of Muly Moluch, like that of Morat, in "Aureng-Zebe," to which it bears a strong resemblance, was admirably represented by Kynaston; who had, says Cibber, "a fierce lion-like majesty in his port and utterance, that gave the spectator a kind of trembling admiration." It is enough to say of Benducar, that the cool, fawning, intriguing, and unprincipled statesman, is fully developed in his whole conduct; and of Alvarez, that the little he has to say and do, is so said and done, as not to disgrace his common-place character of the possessor of the secret on which the plot depends; for it may be casually observed, that the depositary of such a clew to the catastrophe, though of the last importance to the plot, is seldom himself of any interest whatever. The haughty and high-spirited Almeyda is designed by the author as the counterpart of Sebastian. She breaks out with the same violence, I had almost said fury, and frequently discovers a sort of kindred sentiment, intended to prepare the reader for the unfortunate discovery, that she is the sister of the Portuguese monarch.

Of the diction, Dr Johnson has said, with meagre commendation, that it has "some sentiments which leave a strong impression," and "others of excellence, universally acknowledged." This, even when the admiration of the scene betwixt Dorax and Sebastian has been sanctioned by that great critic, seems scanty applause for the chef d'oeuvre of Dryden's dramatic works. The reader will be disposed to look for more unqualified praise, when such a poet was induced, by every pressing consideration, to combine, in one effort, the powers of his mighty genius, and the fruits of his long theatrical experience: Accordingly, Shakespeare laid aside, it will be perhaps difficult to point out a play containing more animatory incident, impassioned language, and beautiful description, than "Don Sebastian." Of the former, the scene betwixt Dorax and the king, had it been the only one ever Dryden wrote, would have been sufficient to insure his immortality. There is not,—no, perhaps, not even in Shakespeare,—an instance where the chord, which the poet designed should vibrate, is more happily struck; strains there are of a higher mood, but not more correctly true; in evidence of which, we have known those, whom distresses of a gentler nature were unable to move, feel their stubborn feelings roused and melted by the injured pride and deep repentance of Dorax. The burst of anguish with which he answers the stern taunt of Sebastian, is one of those rare, but natural instances, in which high-toned passion assumes a figurative language, because all that is familiar seems inadequate to express its feelings:

DORAX
Thou hast dared
To tell me, what I durst not tell myself:
I durst not think that I was spurned, and live;
And live to hear it boasted to my face.
All my long avarice of honour lost,
Heaped up in youth, and hoarded up for age!
Has honour's fountain then sucked back the stream?
He has; and hooting boys may dry-shod pass,
And gather pebbles from the naked ford.
Give me my love, my honour; give them back—
Give me revenge, while I have breath to ask it!

But I will not dwell on the beauties of this scene. If any one is incapable of relishing it, he may safely conclude, that nature has not merely denied him that rare gift, poetical taste, but common powers of comprehending the ordinary feelings of humanity. The love scene, betwixt Sebastian and Almeyda, is more purely conceived, and expressed with more reference to sentiment, than is common with our author. The description which Dorax gives of Sebastian, before his appearance, coming from a mortal enemy, at least from one whose altered love was as envenomed as hatred, is a grand preparation for the appearance of the hero. In many of the slighter descriptive passages, we recognize the poet by those minute touches, which a mind susceptible of poetic feeling is alone capable of bringing out. The approach of the emperor, while the conspirators are caballing, is announced by Orchan, with these picturesque circumstances:

I see the blaze of torches from afar,
And hear the trampling of thick-beating feet—
This way they move.—

The following account, given by the slave sent to observe what passed in the castle of Dorax, believed to be dead, or dying, is equally striking:

HALY
Two hours I warily have watched his palace:
All doors are shut, no servant peeps abroad;
Some officers, with striding haste, past in;
While others outward went on quick dispatch.
Sometimes hushed silence seemed to reign within;
Then cries confused, and a joint clamour followed;
Then lights went gliding by, from room to room,
And shot like thwarting meteors cross the house.
Not daring further to inquire, I came
With speed to bring you this imperfect news.

The description of the midnight insurrection of the rabble is not less impressive:

HAMET
What you wish:
The streets are thicker in this noon of night,
Than at the mid-day sun: A drouzy horror
Sits on their eyes, like fear, not well awake:
All crowd in heaps, as, at a night alarm,
The bees drive out upon each others backs,
T'imboss their hives in clusters; all ask news:
Their busy captain runs the weary round
To whisper orders; and, commanding silence,
Makes not noise cease, but deafens it to murmurs.

These illustrations are designedly selected from the parts of the lower characters, because they at once evince the diligence and success with which Dryden has laboured even the subordinate points of this tragedy.

"Don Sebastian" has been weighed, with reference to its tragic merits, against "Love for Love;" and one or other is universally allowed to be the first of Dryden's dramatic performances. To the youth of both sexes the latter presents the most pleasing subject of emotion; but to those whom age has rendered incredulous upon the romantic effects of love, and who do not fear to look into the recesses of the human heart, when agitated by darker and more stubborn passions, "Don Sebastian" offers a far superior source of gratification.

To point out the blemishes of so beautiful a tragedy, is a painful, though a necessary, task. The style, here and there, exhibits marks of a reviving taste for those frantic bursts of passion, which our author has himself termed the "Dalilahs of the theatre." The first speech of Sebastian has been often noticed as an extravagant rant, more worthy of Maximin, or Almanzor, than of a character drawn by our author in his advanced years, and chastened taste:

I beg no pity for this mouldering clay;
For if you give it burial, there it takes
Possession of your earth:
If burnt and scatter'd in the air, the winds,
That strew my dust, diffuse my royalty,
And spread me o'er your clime; for where one atom
Of mine shall light, know, there Sebastian reigns.

The reader's discernment will discover some similar extravagancies in the language of Almeyda and the Emperor.

It is a separate objection, that the manners of the age and country are not adhered to. Sebastian, by disposition a crusading knight-errant, devoted to religion and chivalry, becomes, in the hands of Dryden, merely a gallant soldier and high-spirited prince, such as existed in the poet's own days. But, what is worse, the manners of Mahometans are shockingly violated. Who ever heard of human sacrifices, or of any sacrifices, being offered up to Mahomet[2]; and when were his followers able to use the classical and learned allusions which occur throughout the dialogue! On this last topic Addison makes the following observations, in the "Guardian," No. 110.

"I have now Mr Dryden's "Don Sebastian" before me, in which I find frequent allusions to ancient poetry, and the old mythology of the heathens. It is not very natural to suppose a king of Portugal would be borrowing thoughts out of Ovid's "Metamorphoses," when he talked even to those of his own court; but to allude to these Roman fables, when he talks to an emperor of Barbary, seems very extraordinary. But observe how he defies him out of the classics in the following lines:

Why didst not thou engage me man to man,
And try the virtue of that Gorgon face,
To stare me into statue?

"Almeyda, at the same time, is more book-learned than Don Sebastian. She plays an Hydra upon the Emperor, that is full as good as the Gorgon:

O that I had the fruitful heads of Hydra,
That one might bourgeon where another fell!
Still would I give thee work, still, still, thou tyrant,
And hiss thee with the last.

"She afterwards, in allusion to Hercules, bids him 'lay down the lion's skin, and take the distaff;' and, in the following speech, utters her passion still more learnedly:

No; were we joined, even though it were in death,
Our bodies burning in one funeral pile,
The prodigy of Thebes would be renewed,
And my divided flame should break from thine.

"The emperor of Barbary shews himself acquainted with the Roman poets as well as either of his prisoners, and answers the foregoing speech in the same classic strain:

Serpent, I will engender poison with thee:
Our offspring, like the seed of dragon's teeth,
Shall issue armed, and fight themselves to death.

"Ovid seems to have been Muley-Moloch's favourite author; witness the lines that follow:

She, still inexorable, still imperious,
And loud, as if, like Bacchus, born in thunder.

"I shall conclude my remarks on his part with that poetical complaint of his being in love; and leave my reader to consider, how prettily it would sound in the mouth of an emperor of Morocco:

The god of love once more has shot his fires
Into my soul, and my whole heart receives him.

"Muley Zeydan is as ingenious a man as his brother Muley Moloch; as where he hints at the story of Castor and Pollux:

May we ne'er meet;
For, like the twins of Leda, when I mount,
He gallops down the skies.

"As for the Mufti, we will suppose that he was bred up a scholar, and not only versed in the law of Mahomet, but acquainted with all kinds of polite learning. For this reason he is not at all surprised when Dorax calls him a Phæton in one place, and in another tells him he is like Archimedes.

"The Mufti afterwards mentions Ximenes, Albornoz, and cardinal Wolsey, by name. The poet seems to think, he may make every person, in his play, know as much as himself, and talk as well as he could have done on the same occasion. At least, I believe, every reader will agree with me, that the above-mentioned sentiments, to which I might have added several others, would have been better suited to the court of Augustus than that of Muley Moloch. I grant they are beautiful in themselves, and much more so in that noble language, which was peculiar to this great poet. I only observe, that they are improper for the persons who make use of them."

The catastrophe of the tragedy may be also censured, not only on the grounds objected to that of "OEdipus," but because it does not naturally flow from the preceding events, and opens, in the fifth act, a new set of persons, and a train of circumstances, unconnected with the preceding action. In the concluding scene, it was remarked, by the critics, that there is a want of pure taste in the lovers dwelling more upon the pleasures than the horrors of their incestuous connection.

Of the lighter scenes, which were intended for comic, Dr Johnson has said, "they are such as that age did not probably commend, and as the present would not endure." Dryden has remarked, with self-complacency, the art with which they are made to depend upon the serious business. This has not, however, the merit of novelty; being not unlike the connection between the tragic and comic scenes of the "Spanish Friar." The persons introduced have also some resemblance; though the gaiety of Antonio is far more gross than that of Lorenzo, and Morayma is a very poor copy of Elvira. It is rather surprising, that when a gay libertine was to be introduced, Dryden did not avail himself of a real character, the English Stukely; a wild gallant, who, after spending a noble fortune, became the leader of a band of Italian Condottieri, engaged in the service of Sebastian, and actually fell in the battle of Alcazar. Collier complains, and with very good reason, that, in the character of the Mufti, Dryden has seized an opportunity to deride and calumniate the priesthood of every religion; an opportunity which, I am sorry to say, he seldom fails to use with unjustifiable inveteracy. The rabble scenes were probably given, as our author himself says of that in Cleomenes, "to gratify the more barbarous part of the audience." Indeed, to judge from the practice of the drama at this time, the representation of a riot upon the stage seems to have had the same charms for the popular part of the English audience, which its reality always possesses in the streets.

Notwithstanding the excellence of this tragedy, it appears to have been endured, rather than applauded, at its first representation; although, being judiciously curtailed, it soon became a great favourite with the public[3]; and, omitting the comic scenes, may be again brought forward with advantage, when the public shall be tired of children and of show. The tragedy of "Don Sebastian" was acted and printed in 1690.

Footnotes

1. "The Battle of Alcazar, with Captain Stukely's death, acted by the Lord High Admiral's servants, 1594," 4to. Baker thinks Dryden might have taken the hint of "Don Sebastian" from this old play. Shakespeare drew from it some of the bouncing rants of Pistol, as, "Feed, and be fat; my fair Callipolis," &c.

2. In a Zambra dance, introduced in the "Conquest of Granada," our author had previously introduced the Moors bowing to the image of Jupiter; a gross solecism, hardly more pardonable, as Langbaine remarks, than the introduction of a pistol in the hand of Demetrius, a successor of Alexander the Great, which Dryden has justly censured.

3. Langbaine says, it was acted "with great applause;" but this must refer to its reception after the first night; for the author's own expressions, that "the audience endured it with much patience, and were weary with much good nature and silence," exclude the idea of a brilliant reception on the first representation. See the beginning of the Preface.

TO THE RIGHT HONOURABLE PHILIP, EARL OF LEICESTER, &c.[1]

Far be it from me, my most noble lord, to think, that any thing which my meanness can produce, should be worthy to be offered to your patronage; or that aught which I can say of you should recommend you farther to the esteem of good men in this present age, or to the veneration which will certainly be paid you by posterity. On the other side, I must acknowledge it a great presumption in me, to make you this address; and so much the greater, because by the common suffrage even of contrary parties, you have been always regarded as one of the first persons of the age, and yet not one writer has dared to tell you so; whether we have been all conscious to ourselves that it was a needless labour to give this notice to mankind, as all men are ashamed to tell stale news; or that we were justly diffident of our own performances, as even Cicero is observed to be in awe when he writes to Atticus; where, knowing himself over-matched in good sense, and truth of knowledge, he drops the gaudy train of words, and is no longer the vain-glorious orator. From whatever reason it may be, I am the first bold offender of this kind: I have broken down the fence, and ventured into the holy grove. How I may be punished for my profane attempt, I know not; but I wish it may not be of ill omen to your lordship: and that a crowd of bad writers do not rush into the quiet of your recesses after me. Every man in all changes of government, which have been, or may possibly arrive, will agree, that I could not have offered my incense, where it could be so well deserved. For you, my lord, are secure in your own merit; and all parties, as they rise uppermost, are sure to court you in their turns; it is a tribute which has ever been paid your virtue. The leading men still bring their bullion to your mint, to receive the stamp of their intrinsic value, that they may afterwards hope to pass with human kind. They rise and fall in the variety of revolutions, and are sometimes great, and therefore wise in men's opinions, who must court them for their interest. But the reputation of their parts most commonly follows their success; few of them are wise, but as they are in power; because indeed, they have no sphere of their own, but, like the moon in the Copernican system of the world, are whirled about by the motion of a greater planet. This it is to be ever busy; neither to give rest to their fellow-creatures, nor, which is more wretchedly ridiculous, to themselves; though, truly, the latter is a kind of justice, and giving mankind a due revenge, that they will not permit their own hearts to be at quiet, who disturb the repose of all beside them. Ambitious meteors! how willing they are to set themselves upon the wing, and taking every occasion of drawing upward to the sun, not considering that they have no more time allowed them for their mounting, than the short revolution of a day; and that when the light goes from them, they are of necessity to fall. How much happier is he, (and who he is I need not say, for there is but one phoenix in an age) who, centering on himself, remains immoveable, and smiles at the madness of the dance about him? he possesses the midst, which is the portion of safety and content. He will not be higher, because he needs it not; but by the prudence of that choice, he puts it out of fortune's power to throw him down. It is confest, that if he had not so been born, he might have been too high for happiness; but not endeavouring to ascend, he secures the native height of his station from envy, and cannot descend from what he is, because he depends not on another. What a glorious character was this once in Rome! I should say, in Athens; when, in the disturbances of a state as mad as ours, the wise Pomponius transported all the remaining wisdom and virtue of his country into the sanctuary of peace and learning. But I would ask the world, (for you, my lord, are too nearly concerned to judge this cause) whether there may not yet be found a character of a noble Englishman, equally shining with that illustrious Roman? Whether I need to name a second Atticus? or whether the world has not already prevented me, and fixed it there, without my naming? Not a second, with a *longo sed proximus intervallo*; not a young Marcellus, flattered by a poet into the resemblance of the first, with a *frons læta parum, et dejecto lumina vultu*, and the rest that follows, *si qua fata aspera rumpas, tu Marcellus eris*; but a person of the same stamp and magnitude, who owes nothing to the former, besides the word Roman, and the superstition of reverence, devolving on him by the precedency of eighteen hundred years; one who walks by him with equal paces, and shares the eyes of beholders with him; one who had been first, had he first lived; and, in spite of doating veneration, is still his equal: both of them born of noble families, in unhappy ages of change and tumult; both of them retiring from affairs of state; yet not leaving the commonwealth, till it had left itself; but never returning to public business, when they had once quitted it, though courted by the heads of either party. But who would trust the quiet of their lives with the extravagancies of their countrymen, when they are just in the giddiness of their turning; when the ground was tottering under them at every moment; and none could guess whether the next heave of the earthquake would settle them on the first foundation, or swallow it? Both of them knew mankind exactly well, for both of them began that study in themselves, and there they found the best part of human composition; the worst they learned by long experience of the folly, ignorance, and immorality of most beside them. Their philosophy, on both sides, was not wholly speculative, for that is barren, and produces nothing but vain ideas of things which cannot possibly be known, or, if they could, yet would only terminate in the understanding; but it was a noble, vigorous and practical philosophy, which exerted itself in all the offices of pity, to those who were unfortunate, and deserved not so to be. The friend was always more considered by them than the cause; and an Octavius, or an Antony in distress, were relieved by them, as well as a Brutus or a Cassius; for the lowermost party, to a noble mind, is ever the fittest object of good-will. The eldest of them, I will suppose, for his honour, to have been of the academic sect, neither dogmatist nor stoick; if he were not, I am sure he ought, in common justice, to yield the precedency to his younger brother. For stiffness of opinion is the effect of pride, and not of philosophy; it is a miserable presumption of that knowledge which human nature is too narrow to contain; and the ruggedness of a stoick is only a silly affectation of being a god,—to wind himself up by pullies to an insensibility of suffering, and, at the same time, to give the lie to his own experience, by saying he suffers not, what he knows he feels. True philosophy is certainly of a more pliant nature, and more accommodated to human use; Homo sum, humani à me nihil alienum puto. A wise man will never attempt an impossibility; and such it is to strain himself beyond the nature of his being, either to become a deity, by being above suffering, or to debase himself into a stock or stone, by pretending not to feel it. To find in ourselves the weaknesses and imperfections of our wretched kind, is surely the most reasonable step we can make towards the compassion of our fellow-creatures. I could give examples of this kind in the second Atticus. In every turn of state, without meddling on either side, he has always been favourable and assisting to oppress merit. The praises which were given by a great poet to the late queen-mother, on her rebuilding Somerset Palace, one part of which was fronting to the mean houses on the other side of the water, are as justly his:

For the distrest and the afflicted lie
Most in his thoughts, and always in his eye[2].

Neither has he so far forgotten a poor inhabitant of his suburbs, whose best prospect is on the garden of Leicester House, but that more than once he has been offering him his patronage, to reconcile him to a world, of which his misfortunes have made him weary[3]. There is another Sidney still remaining, though there can never be another Spenser to deserve the favour. But one Sidney gave his patronage to the applications of a poet; the other offered it unasked. Thus, whether as a second Atticus, or a second Sir Philip Sidney, the latter in all respects will not have the worse of the comparison; and if he will take up with the second place, the world will not so far flatter his modesty, as to seat him there, unless it be out of a deference of manners, that he may place himself where he pleases at his own table.

I may therefore safely conclude, that he, who, by the consent of all men, bears so eminent a character, will out of his inborn nobleness forgive the presumption of this address. It is an unfinished picture, I confess, but the lines and features are so like, that it cannot be mistaken for any other; and without writing any name under it, every beholder must cry out, at first sight,—this was designed for Atticus; but the bad artist has cast too much of him into shades. But I have this excuse, that even the greatest masters commonly fall short of the best faces. They may flatter an indifferent beauty; but the excellencies of nature can have no right done to them; for there both the pencil and pen are overcome by the dignity of the subject; as our admirable Waller has expressed it,

The heroe's race transcends the poet's thought.

There are few in any age who can bear the load of a dedication; for where praise is undeserved, it is satire; though satire on folly is now no longer a scandal to any one person, where a whole age is dipt together. Yet I had rather undertake a multitude one way, than a single Atticus the other; for it is easier to descend than it is to climb. I should have gone ashamed out of the world, if I had not at least attempted this address, which I have long thought owing: and if I had never attempted, I might have been vain enough to think I might have succeeded in it. Now I have made the experiment, and have failed through my unworthiness, I may rest satisfied, that either the adventure is not to be atchieved, or that it is reserved for some other hand.

Be pleased, therefore, since the family of the Attici is and ought to be above the common forms of concluding letters, that I may take my leave in the words of Cicero to the first of them: Me, O Pomponi, valdè pænitet vivere: tantùm te oro, ut quoniam me ipse semper amàsti, ut eodem amore sis; ego nimirum idem sum. Inimici mei mea mihi non meipsum ademerunt. Cura, Attice, ut valeas.

Dabam. Cal.
Jan. 1690.

Footnotes

1. In order to escape as far as possible the odium, which after the Revolution was attached to Dryden's politics and religion, he seems occasionally to have sought for patrons amongst those Nobles of opposite principles, whom moderation, or love of literature, rendered superior to the suggestions of party rancour; or, as he himself has expressed it in the Dedication of "Amphitryon," who, though of a contrary opinion themselves, blamed him not for adhering to a lost cause, and judging for himself what he could not chuse but judge. Philip Sidney, the third earl of Leicester, had taken an active part against the king in the civil wars, had been named one of his judges, though he never took his seat among the regicides, and had been one of Cromwell's Council of State. He was brother of the famous Algernon Sidney, and although retired from party strife, during the violent contests betwixt the Whigs and Tories in 1682-3, there can be no doubt which way his inclinations leaned. He died 6th March, 1696-7, aged more than eighty years. Mr Malone has strongly censured the strain of this Dedication, because it represents Leicester as abstracted from parties and public affairs, notwithstanding his active share in the civil wars. Yet Dryden was not obliged to draw the portrait of his patron from his conduct thirty years before; and if Leicester's character was to be taken from the latter part of his life, surely the praise of moderation is due to him, who, during the factious contests of Charles II's. reign, in which his own brother made so conspicuous a figure, maintained the neutrality of Pomponius Atticus.

2. When Henrietta Maria, widow of Charles I. and queen-dowager of England, visited her son after the Restoration, she chose Somerset-House for her residence, and added all the buildings fronting the river. Cowley, whom she had long patronised, composed a poem on the "Queen's repairing Somerset-House,"

to which our author refers. Mr Malone's accuracy has detected a slight alteration in the verses, as quoted by Dryden, and as written by Cowley:

If any prouder virtuoso's sense
At that part of my prospect take offence,
By which the meaner cabanes are descried
Of my imperial river's humbler side;
If they call that a blemish, let them know,
God and my godlike mistress think not so;
For the distressed and the afflicted lie
Most in their care, and always in their eye.

3. Our poet's house was in Gerard-Street, looking upon the gardens of Leicester-House.

THE PREFACE

Whether it happened through a long disuse of writing, that I forgot the usual compass of a play, or that, by crowding it with characters and incidents, I put a necessity upon myself of lengthening the main action, I know not; but the first day's audience sufficiently convinced me of my error, and that the poem was insupportably too long. It is an ill ambition of us poets, to please an audience with more than they can bear; and supposing that we wrote as well as vainly we imagine ourselves to write, yet we ought to consider, that no man can bear to be long tickled. There is a nauseousness in a city-feast, when we are to sit four hours after we are cloyed. I am therefore, in the first place, to acknowledge, with all manner of gratitude, their civility, who were pleased to endure it with so much patience; to be weary with so much good-nature and silence; and not to explode an entertainment which was designed to please them, or discourage an author, whose misfortunes have once more brought him, against his will, upon the stage. While I continue in these bad circumstances, (and, truly, I see very little probability of coming out) I must be obliged to write; and if I may still hope for the same kind usage, I shall the less repent of that hard necessity. I write not this out of any expectation to be pitied, for I have enemies enow to wish me yet in a worse condition; but give me leave to say, that if I can please by writing, as I shall endeavour it, the town may be somewhat obliged to my misfortunes for a part of their diversion. Having been longer acquainted with the stage than any poet now living, and having observed how difficult it was to please; that the humours of comedy were almost spent; that love and honour (the mistaken topics of tragedy) were quite worn out; that the theatres could not support their charges; that the audience forsook them; that young men, without learning, set up for judges, and that they talked loudest, who understood the least; all these discouragements had not only weaned me from the stage, but had also given me a loathing of it. But enough of this: the difficulties continue; they increase; and I am still condemned to dig in those exhausted mines.

Whatever fault I next commit, rest assured it shall not be that of too much length: Above twelve hundred lines have been cut off from this tragedy since it was first delivered to the actors. They were indeed so judiciously lopped by Mr Betterton, to whose care and excellent action I am equally obliged, that the connection of the story was not lost; but, on the other side, it was impossible to prevent some part of the action from being precipitated, and coming on without that due preparation which is required to all great events: as, in particular, that of raising the mobile, in the beginning of the fourth act, which a man of Benducar's cool character could not naturally attempt, without taking all those precautions, which he foresaw would be necessary to render his design successful. On this consideration, I have replaced those lines through the whole poem, and thereby restored it to that clearness of conception, and (if I may dare to say it) that lustre and masculine vigour, in which it was first written. It is obvious to every understanding reader, that the most poetical parts, which are descriptions, images, similitudes, and moral sentences, are those which of necessity were to be pared away, when the body was swollen into too large a bulk for the representation of the stage. But there is a vast difference betwixt a public entertainment on the theatre, and a private reading in the closet: In the first, we are confined to time; and though we talk not by the hour-glass, yet the watch often drawn out of the pocket warns the actors that their audience is weary; in the last, every reader is judge of his own convenience; he can take up the book and lay it down at his pleasure, and find out those beauties of propriety in thought and writing, which escaped him in the tumult and hurry of representing. And I dare boldly promise for this play, that in the roughness of the numbers and cadences, (which I assure was not casual, but so designed) you will see somewhat more masterly arising to your view, than in most, if not any, of my former tragedies. There is a more noble daring in the figures, and more suitable to the loftiness of the subject; and, besides this, some newnesses of English, translated from the beauties of modern tongues, as well as from the elegancies of the Latin; and here and there some old words are sprinkled, which, for their significance and sound, deserved not to be antiquated; such as we often find in Sallust amongst the Roman authors, and in Milton's "Paradise" amongst ours; though perhaps the latter, instead of sprinkling, has dealt them with too free a hand, even sometimes to the obscuring of his sense.

As for the story, or plot, of the tragedy, it is purely fiction; for I take it up where the history has laid it down. We are assured by all writers of those times, that Sebastian, a young prince of great courage and expectation, undertook that war, partly upon a religious account, partly at the solicitation of Muley Mahomet, who had been driven out of his dominions by Abdelmelech, or, as others call him, Muley Moluch, his nigh kinsman, who descended from the same family of Xeriffs, whose fathers, Hamet and Mahomet, had conquered that empire with joint forces, and shared it betwixt them after their victory; that the body of Don Sebastian was never found in the field of battle, which gave occasion for many to believe, that he was not slain[1]; that some years after, when the Spaniards, with a pretended title, by force of arms, had usurped the crown of Portugal from the house of Braganza, a certain person, who called himself Don Sebastian, and had all the marks of his body and features of his face, appeared at Venice, where he was owned by some of his countrymen; but being seized by the Spaniards, was first imprisoned, then sent to the gallies, and at last put to death in private. It is most certain, that the Portuguese expected his return for almost an age together after that battle, which is at least a proof of their extreme love to his memory; and the usage they had from their new conquerors, might possibly make them so extravagant in their hopes and wishes for their old master[2].

This ground-work the history afforded me, and I desire no better to build a play upon; for where the event of a great action is left doubtful, there the poet is left master. He may raise what he pleases on that foundation, provided he makes it of a piece, and according to the rule of probability. From hence I was only obliged, that Sebastian should return to Portugal no more; but at the same time I had him at my own disposal, whether to bestow him in Afric, or in any other corner of the world, or to have closed the tragedy with his death; and the last of these was certainly the most easy, but for the same reason the least artful; because, as I have somewhere said, the poison and the dagger are still at hand to butcher a hero, when a poet wants the brains to save him. It being therefore only necessary, according to the laws of the drama, that Sebastian should no more be seen upon the throne, I leave it for the world to judge, whether or no I have disposed of him according to art, or have bungled up the conclusion of his adventure. In the drawing of his character, I forgot not piety, which any one may observe to be one principal ingredient of it, even so far as to be a habit in him; though I shew him once to be transported from it by the violence of a sudden passion, to endeavour a self-murder. This being presupposed, that he was religious, the horror of his incest, though innocently committed, was the best reason which the stage could give for hindering his return. It is true, I have no right to blast his memory with such a crime; but declaring it to be fiction, I desire my audience to think it no longer true, than while they are seeing it represented; for that once ended, he may be a saint, for aught I know, and we have reason to presume he is. On this supposition, it was unreasonable to have killed him; for the learned Mr Rymer has well observed, that in all punishments we are to regulate ourselves by poetical justice; and according to those measures, an involuntary sin deserves not death; from whence it follows, that to divorce himself from the beloved object, to retire into a desert, and deprive himself of a throne, was the utmost punishment which a poet could inflict, as it was also the utmost reparation which Sebastian could make. For what relates to Almeyda, her part is wholly fictitious. I know it is the surname of a noble family in Portugal, which was very instrumental in the restoration of Don John de Braganza, father to the most illustrious and most pious princess, our queen-dowager. The French author of a novel, called "Don Sebastian," has given that name to an African lady of his own invention, and makes her sister to Muley Mahomet; but I have wholly changed the accidents, and borrowed nothing but the supposition, that she was beloved by the king of Portugal. Though, if I had taken the whole story, and wrought it up into a play, I might have done it exactly according to the practice of almost all the ancients, who were never accused of being plagiaries for building their tragedies on known fables. Thus, Augustus Cæsar wrote an "Ajax," which was not the less his own, because Euripides had written a play before him on that subject. Thus, of late years, Corneille writ an "OEdipus" after Sophocles; and I have designed one after him, which I wrote with Mr Lee; yet neither the French poet stole from the Greek, nor we from the Frenchman. It is the contrivance, the new turn, and new characters, which alter the property, and make it ours. The materia poetica is as common to all writers, as the materia medica to all physicians. Thus, in our Chronicles, Daniel's history is still his own, though Matthew Paris, Stow, and Hollingshed writ before him; otherwise we must have been content with their dull relations, if a better pen had not been allowed to come after them, and writ his own account after a new and better manner.

I must further declare freely, that I have not exactly kept to the three mechanic rules of unity. I knew them, and had them in my eye, but followed them only at a distance; for the genius of the English cannot bear too regular a play: we are given to variety, even to a debauchery of pleasure. My scenes are therefore sometimes broken, because my underplot required them so to be, though the general scene remains,—of the same castle; and I have taken the time of two days, because the variety of accidents, which are here represented, could not naturally be supposed to arrive in one: but to gain a greater beauty, it is lawful for a poet to supersede a less.

I must likewise own, that I have somewhat deviated from the known history, in the death of Muley Moluch, who, by all relations, died of a fever in the battle, before his army had wholly won the field; but if I have allowed him another day of life, it was because I stood in need of so shining a character of brutality as I have given him; which is indeed the same with that of the present emperor Muley-Ishmael, as some of our English officers, who have been in his court, have credibly informed me.

I have been listening—what objections had been made against the conduct of the play; but found them all so trivial, that if I should name them, a true critic would imagine that I played booty, and only raised up phantoms for myself to conquer. Some are pleased to say—the writing is dull; but, ætatem habet, de se loquatur. Others, that the double poison is unnatural: let the common received opinion, and Ausonius his famous epigram, answer that[3]. Lastly, a more ignorant sort of creatures than either of the former maintain, that the character of Dorax is not only unnatural, but inconsistent with itself: let them read the play, and think again; and if yet they are not satisfied, cast their eyes on that chapter of the wise Montaigne, which is intitled, De l'Inconstance des Actions humaines. A longer reply is what those cavillers deserve not; but I will give them and their fellows to understand, that the earl of Dorset was pleased to read the tragedy twice over before it was acted, and did me the favour to send me word, that I had written beyond any of my former plays, and that he was displeased any thing should be cut away. If I have not reason to prefer his single judgment to a whole faction, let the world be judge; for the opposition is the same with that of Lucan's hero against an army; concurrere bellum, atque virum.

I think I may modestly conclude, that whatever errors there may be, either in the design, or writing of this play, they are not those which have been objected to it. I think also, that I am not yet arrived to the age of doting; and that I have given so much application to this poem, that I could not probably let it run into many gross absurdities; which may caution my enemies from too rash a censure, and may also encourage my friends, who are many more than I could reasonably have expected, to believe their kindness has not been very undeservedly bestowed on me. This is not a play that was huddled up in haste; and, to shew it was not, I will own, that, besides the general moral of it, which is given in the four last lines, there is also another moral, couched under every one of the principal parts and characters, which a judicious critic will observe, though I point not to it in this preface. And there may be also some secret beauties in the decorum of parts, and uniformity of design, which my puny judges will not easily find out: let them consider in the last scene of the fourth act, whether I have not preserved the rule of decency, in giving all the advantage to the royal character, and in making Dorax first submit. Perhaps too they may have thought, that it was through indigence of characters that I have given the same to Sebastian and Almeyda, and consequently made them alike in all things but their sex. But let them look a little deeper into the matter, and they will find, that this identity of character in the greatness of their souls was intended for a preparation of the final discovery, and that the likeness of their nature was a fair hint to the proximity of their blood.

To avoid the imputation of too much vanity, (for all writers, and especially poets, will have some,) I will give but one other instance, in relation to the uniformity of the design. I have observed, that the English will not bear a thorough tragedy; but are pleased, that it should be lightened with underparts of mirth. It had been easy for me to have given my audience a better course of comedy, I mean a more diverting, than that of Antonio and Morayma; but I dare appeal, even to my enemies, if I, or any man, could have invented one, which had been more of a piece, and more depending on the serious part of the design. For what could be more uniform, than to draw from out of the members of a captive court, the subject of a comical entertainment? To prepare this episode, you see Dorax giving the character of Antonio, in the beginning of the play, upon his first sight of him at the lottery; and to make the dependence, Antonio is engaged, in the fourth act, for the deliverance of Almeyda; which is also prepared, by his being first made a slave to the captain of the rabble.

I should beg pardon for these instances; but perhaps they may be of use to future poets, in the conduct of their plays; at least, if I appear too positive, I am growing old, and thereby in possession of some experience, which men in years will always assume for a right of talking. Certainly if a man can ever have reason to set a value on himself, it is when his ungenerous enemies are taking the advantage of the times upon him, to ruin him in his reputation. And therefore, for once, I will make bold to take the counsel of my old master Virgil,

Tu ne cede mails, sed contrà audentior ito.

Footnotes

1. There was a Portuguese prophecy to this purpose, which they applied to the expected return of Sebastian:

Vendra et Incubierto,
Vendra cierto;
Entrera en el huerto,
Per el puerto,
Questa mas a ca del muro;
Y'lo que paresce escuro,
Se vra claro e abierto.

Two false Sebastians, both hermits, laid claim to the throne of Portugal. One was hanged, and the other died in the galleys. Vide Le Quien's Histoire Generale de Portugal.—There are two tracts which appear to regard the last of these impostors, and which may have furnished our author with some slight hints; namely, "The true History of the late and lamentable Adventures of Don Sebastian, King of Portugal, after his imprisonment at Naples until this present day, being now in Spain, at San Lucar de Barrameda.—1602;" and, "A continuation of the lamentable and admirable Adventures of Don Sebastian, King of Portugal, with a Declaration of all his time employed since the Battle in Africk against the Infidels, 1578, until this present year 1603. London, 1603." Both pieces are reprinted in the Harleian Miscellany, Vols IV. and V.

2. The uncertainty of his fate is alluded to by Fletcher:

Wittypate.
In what service have ye been, sir?

Ruinous.
The first that fleshed me a soldier, sir,
Was that great battle at Alcazar, in Barbary,
Where the noble English Stukely fell, and where
The royal Portugal Sebastian ended
His untimely days.

Wittypate.
Are you sure Sebastian died there?

Ruinous.
Faith, sir, there was some other rumour hoped
Amongst us, that he, wounded, escaped, and touched
On his native shore again, where finding his country at home
More distressed by the invasion of the Spaniard
Than his loss abroad, forsook it, still supporting
A miserable and unfortunate life,
Which where he ended is yet uncertain.
Wit at several Weapons.

I have printed this quotation as I find it in the edition of 1778; though I am unable to discover what pretensions it claims to be arranged as blank verse.

3. *Toxica zelotypo dedit uxor mæcha marito,*
Nec satis ad mortem credidit esse datum.
Micuit argenti letalia pondera vivi;
Cogeret ut celerem vis geminata necem.
Dividat hæc si quis, faciunt discreta venenum:
Antidotum sumet, qui sociata bibet.
Ergo inter sese dum noxia pocula certant,
Cessit letalis noxa salutiferæ.
Protinus et vacuos alvi petiere recessus
Lubrica dejectis quà via nota cibis.
Quàm pia cura déum! prodest crudelior uxor,
Et quum fata volunt, bina venena juvant.

PROLOGUE

SENT TO THE AUTHOR BY AN UNKNOWN HAND, AND PROPOSED TO BE SPOKEN BY MRS MOUNTFORD, DRESSED LIKE AN OFFICER[1].

Bright beauties, who in awful circle sit,
And you, grave synod of the dreadful pit,
And you the upper-tire of pop-gun wit,

Pray ease me of my wonder, if you may;
Is all this crowd barely to see the play;
Or is't the poet's execution-day?

His breath is in your hands I will presume,
But I advise you to defer his doom,
Till you have got a better in his room;

And don't maliciously combine together,
As if in spite and spleen you were come hither;
For he has kept the pen, tho' lost the feather[2].

And, on my honour, ladies, I avow,
This play was writ in charity to you;
For such a dearth of wit who ever knew?

Sure 'tis a judgment on this sinful nation,
For the abuse of so great dispensation;
And, therefore, I resolve to change vocation.

For want of petticoat, I've put on buff,

To try what may be got by lying rough:
How think you, sirs? is it not well enough?

Of bully-critics I a troop would lead;
But, one replied,—Thank you, there's no such need,
I at Groom-Porter's, sir, can safer bleed.

Another, who the name of danger loaths,
Vow'd he would go, and swore me forty oaths,
But that his horses were in body-clothes.

A third cried,—Damn my blood, I'll be content
To push my fortune, if the parliament
Would but recal claret from banishment.

A fourth (and I have done) made this excuse—
I'd draw my sword in Ireland, sir, to chuse;
Had not their women gouty legs, and wore no shoes.

Well, I may march, thought I, and fight, and trudge,
But, of these blades, the devil a man will budge;
They there would fight, e'en just as here they judge.

Here they will pay for leave to find a fault;
But, when their honour calls, they can't be bought;
Honour in danger, blood, and wounds is sought.

Lost virtue, whither fled? or where's thy dwelling
Who can reveal? at least, 'tis past my telling,
Unless thou art embarked for Inniskilling.

On carrion-tits those sparks denounce their rage,
In boot of wisp and Leinster frise engage;
What would you do in such an equipage[3]?

The siege of Derry does you gallants threaten;
Not out of errant shame of being beaten,
As fear of wanting meat, or being eaten.

Were wit like honour, to be won by fighting,
How few just judges would there be of writing!
Then you would leave this villainous back-biting.

Your talents lie how to express your spite;
But, where is he who knows to praise aright?
You praise like cowards, but like critics fight.

Ladies, be wise, and wean these yearling calves,

Who, in your service too, are meer faux braves;
They judge, and write, and fight, and love—by halves.

Footnotes

1. The humour of this intended prologue turns upon the unwillingness displayed to attend King William into Ireland by many of the nobility and gentry, who had taken arms at the Revolution. The truth is, that, though invited to go as volunteers, they could not but consider themselves as hostages, of whom William did not chuse to lose sight, lest, while he was conquering Ireland, he might, perchance, lose England, by means of the very men by whom he had won it. The disbanding of the royal regiment had furnished a subject for the satirical wit of Buckingham, at least, such a piece is printed in his Miscellanies; and for that of Shadwell, in his epilogue to Bury-fair. But Shadwell was now poet-laureat, and his satire was privileged, like the wit of the ancient royal jester. Our author was suspected of disaffection, and liable to misconstruction: For which reason, probably, he declined this sarcastic prologue, and substituted that which follows, the tone of which is submissive, and conciliatory towards the government. Contrary to custom, it was spoken by a woman.

2. In allusion to his being deprived of the office of poet laureat.

3. The Inniskilling horse, who behaved with great courage against King James, joined Schomberg and King William's forces at Dundalk, in 1689, rather resembled a foreign frey-corps, than regular troops. "They were followed by multitudes of their women; they were uncouth in their appearance; they rode on small horses, called Garrons; their pistols were not fixed in holsters, but dangled about their persons, being slung to their sword-belts; they offered, with spirit, to make always the forlorn of the army; but, upon the first order they received, they cried out, 'They could thrive no longer, since they were now put under orders.'—Memoirs, Vol. II. p. 133. The allusion in the next verse is to the dreadful siege of Londonderry, when the besieged suffered the last extremities of famine. The account of this memorable leaguer, by the author just quoted, is a most spirited piece of historical painting.

PROLOGUE, SPOKEN BY A WOMAN.

The judge removed, though he's no more my lord,
May plead at bar, or at the council-board:
So may cast poets write; there's no pretension
To argue loss of wit, from loss of pension.
Your looks are chearful; and in all this place
I see not one that wears a damning face.
The British nation is too brave, to show
Ignoble vengeance on a vanquished foe.
At last be civil to the wretch imploring;
And lay your paws upon him, without roaring.
Suppose our poet was your foe before,
Yet now, the business of the field is o'er;
'Tis time to let your civil wars alone,
When troops are into winter-quarters gone.

Jove was alike to Latian and to Phrygian;
And you well know, a play's of no religion.
Take good advice, and please yourselves this day;
No matter from what hands you have the play.
Among good fellows every health will pass,
That serves to carry round another glass:
When with full bowls of Burgundy you dine,
Though at the mighty monarch you repine,
You grant him still Most Christian in his wine.
Thus far the poet; but his brains grow addle,
And all the rest is purely from this noddle.
You have seen young ladies at the senate-door,
Prefer petitions, and your grace implore;
However grave the legislators were,
Their cause went ne'er the worse for being fair.
Reasons as weak as theirs, perhaps, I bring;
But I could bribe you with as good a thing.
I heard him make advances of good nature;
That he, for once, would sheath his cutting satire.
Sign but his peace, he vows he'll ne'er again
The sacred names of fops and beaus profane.
Strike up the bargain quickly; for I swear,
As times go now, he offers very fair.
Be not too hard on him with statutes neither;
Be kind; and do not set your teeth together,
To stretch the laws, as coblers do their leather.
Horses by Papists are not to be ridden,
But sure the muses' horse was ne'er forbidden;
For in no rate-book it was ever found
That Pegasus was valued at five pound[1]:
Fine him to daily drudging and inditing:
And let him pay his taxes out in writing.

Footnote

1. Alluding to the act for disarming the Catholics, by which, inter alia, it is enacted, "that no Papist, or reputed Papist, so refusing, or making default, as aforesaid, at any time after the 15th of May, 1689, shall, or may have, and keep in his own possession, or in the possession of any other person for his use, or at his disposition, any horse or horses, which shall be above the value of L.5."—1st William and Mary, c. 15.

DRAMATIS PERSONÆ

Don SEBASTIAN, King of Portugal.
MULEY-MOLUCH, Emperor of Barbary.

DORAX, a noble Portuguese, now a renegade; formerly Don ALONZO DE SYLVERA, Alcade, or Governor of Alcazar.
BENDUCAR, chief Minister, and favourite to the Emperor.
The Mufti ABDALLA.
MULEY-ZEYDAN, brother to the Emperor.
Don ANTONIO, a young, noble, amorous Portuguese; now a slave.
Don ALVAREZ, an old counsellor to Don SEBASTIAN; now a slave also.
MUSTAPHA, Captain of the Rabble.
Two Merchants.
Rabble.
A Servant to BENDUCAR.
A Servant to the Mufti.

ALMEYDA, a captive Queen of Barbary.
MORAYMA, daughter to the Mufti.
JOHAYMA, chief wife to the Mufti.

SCENE—In the Castle of Alcazar.

DON SEBASTIAN, KING OF PORTUGAL.

ACT I

SCENE I

The scene at Alcazar, representing a market-place under the Castle.

[Enter **MULEY-ZEYDAN** and **BENDUCAR**.

MULEY-ZEYDAN
Now Africa's long wars are at an end,
And our parched earth is drenched in Christian blood;
My conquering brother will have slaves enow,
To pay his cruel vows for victory.—
What hear you of Sebastian, king of Portugal?

BENDUCAR
He fell among a heap of slaughtered Moors,
Though yet his mangled carcase is not found.
The rival of our threatened empire, Mahomet,
Was hot pursued; and, in the general rout,
Mistook a swelling current for a ford,
And in Mucazar's flood was seen to rise:
Thrice was he seen: At length his courser plunged,

And threw him off; the waves whelmed over him,
And, helpless, in his heavy arms he drowned.

MULEY-ZEYDAN
Thus, then, a doubtful title is extinguished;
Thus Moluch, still the favourite of fate,
Swims in a sanguine torrent to the throne,
As if our prophet only worked for him:
The heavens, and all the stars, are his hired servants;
As Muley-Zeydan were not worth their care,
And younger brothers but the draff of nature.

BENDUCAR
Be still, and learn the soothing arts of court:
Adore his fortune, mix with flattering crowds;
And, when they praise him most, be you the loudest.
Your brother is luxurious, close, and cruel;
Generous by fits, but permanent in mischief.
The shadow of a discontent would ruin us;
We must be safe, before we can be great.
These things observed, leave me to shape the rest.

MULEY-ZEYDAN
You have the key; he opens inward to you.

BENDUCAR
So often tried, and ever found so true,
Has given me trust; and trust has given me means
Once to be false for all. I trust not him;
For, now his ends are served, and he grown absolute,
How am I sure to stand, who served those ends?
I know your nature open, mild, and grateful:
In such a prince the people may be blest,
And I be safe.

MULEY-ZEYDAN
My father!

[Embracing him.

BENDUCAR
My future king, auspicious Muley-Zeydan!
Shall I adore you?—No, the place is public:
I worship you within; the outward act
Shall be reserved till nations follow me,
And heaven shall envy you the kneeling world.—
You know the alcade of Alcazar, Dorax?

MULEY-ZEYDAN
The gallant renegade you mean?

BENDUCAR
The same.
That gloomy outside, like a rusty chest,
Contains the shining treasure, of a soul
Resolved and brave: He has the soldiers' hearts,
And time shall make him ours.

MULEY-ZEYDAN
He's just upon us.

BENDUCAR
I know him from afar,
By the long stride, and by the sullen port.—
Retire, my lord.
Wait on your brother's triumph; yours is next:
His growth is but a wild and fruitless plant;
I'll cut his barren branches to the stock,
And graft you on to bear.

MULEY-ZEYDAN
My oracle!

[Exit **MULEY-ZEYDAN**

BENDUCAR
Yes, to delude your hopes.—Poor credulous fool!
To think that I would give away the fruit
Of so much toil, such guilt, and such damnation!
If I am damned, it shall be for myself.
This easy fool must be my stale, set up
To catch the people's eyes: He's tame and merciful;
Him I can manage, till I make him odious
By some unpopular act; and then dethrone him.

[Enter **DORAX**.

Now, Dorax.

DORAX
Well, Benducar.

BENDUCAR
Bare Benducar!

DORAX

Thou would'st have titles; take them then,—chief minister,
First hangman of the state.

BENDUCAR
Some call me, favourite.

DORAX
What's that?—his minion?—
Thou art too old to be a catamite!—
Now pr'ythee tell me, and abate thy pride,
Is not Benducar, bare, a better name
In a friend's mouth, than all those gaudy titles,
Which I disdain to give the man I love?

BENDUCAR
But always out of humour,—

DORAX
I have cause:
Though all mankind is cause enough for satire.

BENDUCAR
Why, then, thou hast revenged thee on mankind.
They say, in fight, thou hadst a thirsty sword,
And well 'twas glutted there.

DORAX
I spitted frogs; I crushed a heap of emmets;
A hundred of them to a single soul,
And that but scanty weight too. The great devil
Scarce thanked me for my pains; he swallows vulgar
Like whipped cream,—feels them not in going down.

BENDUCAR
Brave renegade!—Could'st thou not meet Sebastian?
Thy master had been worthy of thy sword.

DORAX
My master!—By what title?
Because I happened to be born where he
Happened to be king?—And yet I served him;
Nay, I was fool enough to love him too.—
You know my story, how I was rewarded
For fifteen hard campaigns, still hooped in iron,
And why I turned Mahometan. I'm grateful;
But whosoever dares to injure me,
Let that man know, I dare to be revenged.

BENDUCAR
Still you run off from bias:—Say, what moves
Your present spleen?

DORAX
You marked not what I told you.
I killed not one that was his maker's image;
I met with none but vulgar two-legged brutes:
Sebastian was my aim; he was a man:
Nay,—though he hated me, and I hate him,
Yet I must do him right,—he was a man,
Above man's height, even towering to divinity:
Brave, pious, generous, great, and liberal;
Just as the scales of heaven, that weigh the seasons.
He loved his people; him they idolized;
And thence proceeds my mortal hatred to him;
That, thus unblameable to all besides,
He erred to me alone:
His goodness was diffused to human kind,
And all his cruelty confined to me.

BENDUCAR
You could not meet him then?

DORAX
No, though I sought
Where ranks fell thickest.—'Twas indeed the place
To seek Sebastian.—Through a track of death
I followed him, by groans of dying foes;
But still I came too late; for he was flown,
Like lightning, swift before me to new slaughters.
I mowed across, and made irregular harvest,
Defaced the pomp of battle, but in vain;
For he was still supplying death elsewhere.
This mads me, that perhaps ignoble hands
Have overlaid him,—for they could not conquer:
Murdered by multitudes, whom I alone
Had right to slay. I too would have been slain;
That, catching hold upon his flitting ghost,
I might have robbed him of his opening heaven,
And dragged him down with me, spite of predestination.

BENDUCAR
'Tis of as much import as Africk's worth,
To know what came of him, and of Almeyda,
The sister of the vanquished Mahomet,
Whose fatal beauty to her brother drew
The land's third part, as Lucifer did heaven's.

DORAX
I hope she died in her own female calling,
Choked up with man, and gorged with circumcision.
As for Sebastian, we must search the field;
And, where we see a mountain of the slain,
Send one to climb, and, looking down below,
There he shall find him at his manly length,
With his face up to heaven, in the red monument,
Which his true sword has digged.

BENDUCAR
Yet we may possibly hear farther news;
For, while our Africans pursued the chace,
The captain of the rabble issued out,
With a black shirtless train, to spoil the dead,
And seize the living.

DORAX
Each of them an host,
A million strong of vermin every villain:
No part of government, but lords of anarchy,
Chaos of power, and privileged destruction.

BENDUCAR
Yet I must tell you, friend, the great must use them
Sometimes, as necessary tools of tumult.

DORAX
I would use them
Like dogs in times of plague; outlaws of nature,
Fit to be shot and brained, without a process,
To stop infection; that's their proper death.

BENDUCAR
No more;—
Behold the emperor coming to survey
The slaves, in order to perform his vow.

[Enter **MULEY-MOLUCH** the **EMPEROR**, with **ATTENDANTS**; the **MUFTI**, and **MULEY-ZEYDAN**.

MULEY-MOLUCH
Our armours now may rust; our idle scymiters
Hang by our sides for ornament, not use:
Children shall beat our atabals and drums,
And all the noisy trades of war no more
Shall wake the peaceful morn; the Xeriff's blood
No longer in divided channels runs,

The younger house took end in Mahomet:
Nor shall Sebastian's formidable name
Be longer used to lull the crying babe.

MUFTI
For this victorious day, our mighty prophet
Expects your gratitude, the sacrifice
Of Christian slaves, devoted, if you won.

MULEY-MOLUCH
The purple present shall be richly paid;
That vow performed, fasting shall be abolished;
None e'er served heaven well with a starved face:
Preach abstinence no more; I tell thee, Mufti,
Good feasting is devout; and thou, our head,
Hast a religious, ruddy countenance.
We will have learned luxury; our lean faith
Gives scandal to the christians; they feed high:
Then look for shoals of converts, when thou hast
Reformed us into feasting.

MUFTI
Fasting is but the letter of the law,
Yet it shews well to preach it to the vulgar;
Wine is against our law; that's literal too,
But not denied to kings and to their guides;
Wine is a holy liquor for the great.

DORAX [Aside.]
This Mufti, in my conscience, is some English renegado, he talks so savourily of toping.

MULEY-MOLUCH
Bring forth the unhappy relicks of the war.

[Enter **MUSTAPHA**, Captain of the Rabble, with his followers of the **BLACK GUARD**, &c. and other **MOORS**; With them a Company of Portuguese **SLAVES**, without any of the chief Persons.

MULEY-MOLUCH
These are not fit to pay an emperor's vow;
Our bulls and rams had been more noble victims:
These are but garbage, not a sacrifice.

MUFTI
The prophet must not pick and chuse his offerings;
Now he has given the day, 'tis past recalling,
And he must be content with such as these.

MULEY-MOLUCH

But are these all? Speak you, that are their masters.

MUSTAPHA
All, upon my honour; if you will take them as their fathers got them, so; if not, you must stay till they get a better generation. These christians are mere bunglers; they procreate nothing but out of their own wives, and these have all the looks of eldest sons.

MULEY-MOLUCH
Pain of your lives, let none conceal a slave.

MUSTAPHA
Let every man look to his own conscience; I am sure mine shall never hang me.

BENDUCAR
Thou speak'st as if thou wert privy to concealments; then thou art an accomplice.

MUSTAPHA
Nay, if accomplices must suffer, it may go hard with me: but here's the devil on't, there's a great man, and a holy man too, concerned with me; now, if I confess, he'll be sure to escape between his greatness and his holiness, and I shall be murdered, because of my poverty and rascality.

MUFTI [Winking at him.]
Then, if thy silence save the great and holy,
'Tis sure thou shalt go straight to paradise.

MUSTAPHA
'Tis a fine place, they say; but, doctor, I am not worthy on't. I am contented with this homely world; 'tis good enough for such a poor, rascally Mussulman, as I am; besides, I have learnt so much good manners, doctor, as to let my betters be served before me.

MULEY-MOLUCH
Thou talk'st as if the Mufti were concerned.

MUSTAPHA
Your majesty may lay your soul on't. But, for my part, though I am a plain fellow, yet I scorn to be tricked into paradise; I would he should know it. The truth on't is, an't like you, his reverence bought of me the flower of all the market: these—these are but dogs-meat to them; and a round price he paid me, too, I'll say that for him; but not enough for me to venture my neck for. If I get paradise when my time comes, I can't help myself; but I'll venture nothing before-hand, upon a blind bargain.

MULEY-MOLUCH
Where are those slaves? produce them.

MUFTI
They are not what he says.

MULEY-MOLUCH
No more excuses.

[One goes out to fetch them.

Know, thou may'st better dally
With a dead prophet, than a living king.

MUFTI
I but reserved them to present thy greatness
An offering worthy thee.

MUSTAPHA
By the same token there was a dainty virgin, (virgin, said I! but I wont be too positive of that, neither) with a roguish leering eye! he paid me down for her upon the nail a thousand golden sultanins, or he had never had her, I can tell him that; now, is it very likely he would pay so dear for such a delicious morsel, and give it away out of his own mouth, when it had such a farewell with it too?

[Enter **SEBASTIAN**, conducted in mean Habit, with **ALVAREZ, ANTONIO**, and **ALMEYDA**, her Face veiled with a Barnus.

MULEY-MOLUCH
Ay; these look like the workmanship of heaven;
This is the porcelain clay of human kind,
And therefore cast into these noble moulds.

DORAX
By all my wrongs,
[Aside, while the **EMPEROR** whispers **BENDUCAR**.
'Tis he! damnation seize me, but 'tis he!
My heart heaves up and swells; he's poison to me;
My injured honour, and my ravished love,
Bleed at their murderer's sight.

BENDUCAR [Aside to **DORAX**]
The emperor would learn these prisoners' names;
You know them?

DORAX
Tell him, no;
And trouble me no more—I will not know them.
Shall I trust heaven, that heaven which I renounced,
With my revenge? Then, where's my satisfaction?
No; It must be my own, I scorn a proxy. [Aside.

MULEY-MOLUCH
'Tis decreed;
These of a better aspect, with the rest,
Shall share one common doom, and lots decide it.
For every numbered captive, put a ball

Into an urn; three only black be there,
The rest, all white, are safe.

MUFTI
Hold, sir; the woman must not draw.

MULEY-MOLUCH
O Mufti,
We know your reason; let her share the danger.

MUFTI
Our law says plainly, women have no souls.

MULEY-MOLUCH
'Tis true; their souls are mortal, set her by;
Yet, were Almeyda here, though fame reports her
The fairest of her sex, so much, unseen,
I hate the sister of our rival-house,
Ten thousand such dry notions of our Alcoran
Should not protect her life, if not immortal;
Die as she could, all of a piece, the better
That none of her remain.

[Here an Urn is brought in; the Prisoners approach with great concernment, and among the rest, **SEBASTIAN**, **ALVAREZ**, and **ANTONIO**, who come more chearfully.

DORAX
Poor abject creatures, how they fear to die!
These never knew one happy hour in life,
Yet shake to lay it down. Is load so pleasant?
Or has heaven hid the happiness of death,
That men may dare to live?—Now for our heroes.

[The **THREE** approach.

O, these come up with spirits more resolved.
Old venerable Alvarez;—well I know him,
The favourite once of this Sebastian's father;
Now minister, (too honest for his trade)
Religion bears him out; a thing taught young,
In age ill practised, yet his prop in death.
O, he has drawn a black; and smiles upon't,
As who should say,—My faith and soul are white,
Though my lot swarthy: Now, if there be hereafter,
He's blest; if not, well cheated, and dies pleased.

ANTONIO [Holding his lot in his clenched hand.]
Here I have thee;

Be what thou wilt, I will not look too soon:
Thou hast a colour; if thou prov'st not right,
I have a minute good ere I behold thee.
Now, let me roll and grubble thee:
Blind men say, white feels smooth, and black feels rough;
Thou hast a rugged skin, I do not like thee.

DORAX
There's the amorous airy spark, Antonio,
The wittiest woman's toy in Portugal:
Lord, what a loss of treats and serenades!
The whole she-nation will be in mourning for him.

ANTONIO
I've a moist sweaty palm; the more's my sin:
If it be black, yet only dyed, not odious
Damned natural ebony, there's hope, in rubbing,
To wash this Ethiop white.—

[Looks.]

Pox o'the proverb!
As black as hell;—another lucky saying!
I think the devil's in me;—good again!
I cannot speak one syllable, but tends
To death or to damnation.

[Holds up his ball.

DORAX
He looks uneasy at his future journey, [Aside.
And wishes his boots off again, for fear
Of a bad road, and a worse inn at night.
Go to bed, fool, and take secure repose,
For thou shalt wake no more.

[**SEBASTIAN** comes up to draw.

MULEY-MOLUCH [To **BENDUCAR**]
Mark him, who now approaches to the lottery:
He looks secure of death, superior greatness,
Like Jove, when he made Fate, and said, Thou art
The slave of my creation.—I admire him.

BENDUCAR
He looks as man was made; with face erect,
That scorns his brittle corpse, and seems ashamed
He's not all spirit; his eyes, with a dumb pride,

Accusing fortune that he fell not warm;
Yet now disdains to live.

[**SEBASTIAN** draws a black.

MULEY-MOLUCH
He has his wish;
And I have failed of mine.

DORAX
Robbed of my vengeance, by a trivial chance! [Aside.
Fine work above, that their anointed care
Should die such little death! or did his genius
Know mine the stronger dæmon, feared the grapple,
And looking round him, found this nook of fate,
To skulk behind my sword?—Shall I discover him?—
Still he would not die mine; no thanks to my
Revenge; reserved but to more royal shambles.
'Twere base, too, and below those vulgar souls,
That shared his danger, yet not one disclosed him,
But, struck with reverence, kept an awful silence.
I'll see no more of this;—dog of a prophet!

[Exit **DORAX**.

MULEY-MOLUCH
One of these three is a whole hecatomb,
And therefore only one of them shall die:
The rest are but mute cattle; and when death
Comes like a rushing lion, couch like spaniels,
With lolling tongues, and tremble at the paw:
Let lots again decide it.

[The **THREE** draw again; and the Lot falls on **SEBASTIAN**.

SEBASTIAN
Then there's no more to manage: if I fall,
It shall be like myself; a setting sun
Should leave a track of glory in the skies.—
Behold Sebastian, king of Portugal.

MULEY-MOLUCH
Sebastian! ha! it must be he; no other
Could represent such suffering majesty.
I saw him, as he terms himself, a sun
Struggling in dark eclipse, and shooting day
On either side of the black orb that veiled him.

SEBASTIAN
Not less even in this despicable now,
Than when my name filled Afric with affright,
And froze your hearts beneath your torrid zone.

BENDUCAR [To **MULEY-MOLUCH**]
Extravagantly brave! even to an impudence
Of greatness.

SEBASTIAN
Here satiate all your fury:
Let fortune empty her whole quiver on me;
I have a soul, that, like an ample shield,
Can take in all, and verge enough for more.
I would have conquered you; and ventured only
A narrow neck of land for a third world,
To give my loosened subjects room to play.
Fate was not mine,
Nor am I fate's. Now I have pleased my longing,
And trod the ground which I beheld from far,
I beg no pity for this mouldering clay;
For, if you give it burial, there it takes
Possession of your earth;
If burnt and scattered in the air, the winds,
That strow my dust, diffuse my royalty,
And spread me o'er your clime: for where one atom
Of mine shall light, know, there Sebastian reigns.

MULEY-MOLUCH
What shall I do to conquer thee?

SEBASTIAN
Impossible!
Souls know no conquerors.

MULEY-MOLUCH
I'll shew thee for a monster through my Afric.

SEBASTIAN
No, thou canst only shew me for a man:
Afric is stored with monsters; man's a prodigy,
Thy subjects have not seen.

MULEY-MOLUCH
Thou talk'st as if
Still at the head of battle.

SEBASTIAN

Thou mistakest,
For then I would not talk.

BENDUCAR
Sure he would sleep.

SEBASTIAN
Till doomsday, when the trumpet sounds to rise;
For that's a soldier's call.

MULEY-MOLUCH
Thou'rt brave too late;
Thou shouldst have died in battle, like a soldier.

SEBASTIAN
I fought and fell like one, but death deceived me;
I wanted weight of feeble Moors upon me,
To crush my soul out.

MULEY-MOLUCH
Still untameable!
In what a ruin has thy head-strong pride,
And boundless thirst of empire, plunged thy people!

SEBASTIAN
What sayst thou? ha! no more of that.

MULEY-MOLUCH
Behold,
What carcases of thine thy crimes have strewed,
And left our Afric vultures to devour.

BENDUCAR
Those souls were those thy God intrusted with thee,
To cherish, not destroy.

SEBASTIAN
Witness, O heaven, how much
This sight concerns me! would I had a soul
For each of these; how gladly would I pay
The ransom down! But since I have but one,
'Tis a king's life, and freely 'tis bestowed.
Not your false prophet, but eternal justice
Has destined me the lot, to die for these:
'Tis fit a sovereign so should pay such subjects;
For subjects such as they are seldom seen,
Who not forsook me at my greatest need;
Nor for base lucre sold their loyalty,

But shared my dangers to the last event,
And fenced them with their own. These thanks I pay you;

[Wipes his eyes.

And know, that, when Sebastian weeps, his tears
Come harder than his blood.

MULEY-MOLUCH
They plead too strongly
To be withstood. My clouds are gathering too,
In kindly mixture with his royal shower.
Be safe; and owe thy life, not to my gift,
But to the greatness of thy mind, Sebastian.
Thy subjects too shall live; a due reward
For their untainted faith, in thy concealment.

MUFTI
Remember, sir, your vow.

[A general shout.

MULEY-MOLUCH
Do thou remember
Thy function, mercy, and provoke not blood.

MUFTI
One of his generous fits, too strong to last.

[Aside to **BENDUCAR**.

BENDUCAR
The Mufti reddens; mark that holy cheek. [To him.
He frets within, froths treason at his mouth,
And churns it thro' his teeth; leave me to work him.

SEBASTIAN
A mercy unexpected, undesired,
Surprises more: you've learnt the art to vanquish.
You could not,—give me leave to tell you, sir,—
Have given me life but in my subjects' safety:
Kings, who are fathers, live but in their people.

MULEY-MOLUCH
Still great, and grateful; that's thy character.—
Unveil the woman; I would view the face,
That warmed our Mufti's zeal:
These pious parrots peck the fairest fruit:

Such tasters are for kings.

[Officers go to **ALMEYDA** to unveil her.

ALMEYDA
Stand off, ye slaves! I will not be unveiled.

MULEY-MOLUCH
Slave is thy title:—force her.

SEBASTIAN
On your lives, approach her not.

MULEY-MOLUCH
How's this!

SEBASTIAN
Sir, pardon me,
And hear me speak.—

ALMEYDA
Hear me; I will be heard.
I am no slave; the noblest blood of Afric
Runs in my veins; a purer stream than thine:
For, though derived from the same source, thy current
Is puddled and defiled with tyranny.

MULEY-MOLUCH
What female fury have we here!

ALMEYDA
I should be one,
Because of kin to thee. Wouldst thou be touched
By the presuming hands of saucy grooms?
The same respect, nay more, is due to me:
More for my sex; the same for my descent.
These hands are only fit to draw the curtain.
Now, if thou dar'st, behold Almeyda's face.

[Unveils herself.

BENDUCAR
Would I had never seen it! [Aside.

ALMEYDA
She whom thy Mufti taxed to have no soul;
Let Afric now be judge.
Perhaps thou think'st I meanly hope to 'scape,

As did Sebastian, when he owned his greatness.
But to remove that scruple, know, base man,
My murdered father, and my brother's ghost,
Still haunt this breast, and prompt it to revenge.
Think not I could forgive, nor dar'st thou pardon.

MULEY-MOLUCH
Wouldst thou revenge thee, trait'ress, hadst thou power?

ALMEYDA
Traitor, I would; the name's more justly thine;
Thy father was not, more than mine, the heir
Of this large empire: but with arms united
They fought their way, and seized the crown by force;
And equal as their danger was their share:
For where was eldership, where none had right
But that which conquest gave? 'Twas thy ambition
Pulled from my peaceful father what his sword
Helped thine to gain; surprised him and his kingdom,
No provocation given, no war declared.

MULEY-MOLUCH
I'll hear no more.

ALMEYDA
This is the living coal, that, burning in me,
Would flame to vengeance, could it find a vent;
My brother too, that lies yet scarcely cold
In his deep watery bed;—my wandering mother,
Who in exile died—
O that I had the fruitful heads of Hydra,
That one might bourgeon where another fell!
Still would I give thee work; still, still, thou tyrant,
And hiss thee with the last.

MULEY-MOLUCH
Something, I know not what, comes over me:
Whether the toils of battle, unrepaired
With due repose, or other sudden qualm.—
Benducar, do the rest.

[Goes off, the court follows him.

BENDUCAR
Strange! in full health! this pang is of the soul;
The body's unconcerned: I'll think hereafter.—
Conduct these royal captives to the castle;
Bid Dorax use them well, till further order.

[Going off, stops.

The inferior captives their first owners take,
To sell, or to dispose.—You Mustapha,
Set ope the market for the sale of slaves.

[Exit BENDUCAR.

[The **MASTERS** and **SLAVES** come forward, and **BUYERS** of several Qualities come in, and chaffer about the several **OWNERS**, who make their **SLAVES** do Tricks[1].

MUSTAPHA
My chattels are come into my hands again, and my conscience will serve me to sell them twice over; any price now, before the Mufti come to claim them.

1st MERCHANT [To **MUSTAPHA**.]
What dost hold that old fellow at?—

[Pointing to **ALVAREZ**.]

He's tough, and has no service in his limbs.

MUSTAPHA
I confess he's somewhat tough; but I suppose you would not boil him, I ask for him a thousand crowns.

1st MERCHANT
Thou mean'st a thousand marvedis.

MUSTAPHA
Pr'ythee, friend, give me leave to know my own meaning.

1st MERCHANT
What virtues has he to deserve that price?

MUSTAPHA
Marry come up, sir! virtues, quotha! I took him in the king's company; he's of a great family, and rich; what other virtues wouldst thou have in a nobleman?

1st MERCHANT
I buy him with another man's purse, that's my comfort. My lord Dorax, the governor, will have him at any rate:—There's hansel. Come, old fellow, to the castle.

ALVAREZ
To what is miserable age reserved! [Aside.
But oh the king! and oh the fatal secret!
Which I have kept thus long to time it better,
And now I would disclose, 'tis past my power.

[Exit with his **MASTER**.

MUSTAPHA
Something of a secret, and of the king, I heard him mutter: a pimp, I warrant him, for I am sure he is an old courtier. Now, to put off t'other remnant of my merchandize.—Stir up, sirrah!   [To **ANTONIO**.

ANTONIO
Dog, what wouldst thou have?

MUSTAPHA
Learn better manners, or I shall serve you a dog-trick; come down upon all-four immediately; I'll make you know your rider.

ANTONIO
Thou wilt not make a horse of me?

MUSTAPHA
Horse or ass, that's as thy mother made thee: but take earnest, in the first place, for thy sauciness.—

[Lashes him with his Whip.]

—Be advised, friend, and buckle to thy geers: Behold my ensign of royalty displayed over thee.

ANTONIO
I hope one day to use thee worse in Portugal.

MUSTAPHA
Ay, and good reason, friend; if thou catchest me a-conquering on thy side of the water, lay on me lustily; I will take it as kindly as thou dost this.—

[Holds up his Whip.

ANTONIO [Lying down.]
Hold, my dear Thrum-cap: I obey thee cheerfully.—I see the doctrine of non-resistance is never practiced thoroughly, but when a man can't help himself.

[Enter a **SECOND MERCHANT**.

2ND MERCHANT
You, friend, I would see that fellow do his postures.

MUSTAPHA [Bridling **ANTONIO**.]
Now, sirrah, follow, for you have rope enough: To your paces, villain, amble trot, and gallop:—Quick about, there.—Yeap! the more money's bidden for you, the more your credit.

[**ANTONIO** follows, at the end of the Bridle, on his Hands and Feet, and does all his Postures.

2ND MERCHANT
He is well chined, and has a tolerable good back; that is half in half.—[To **MUSTAPHA**.]—I would see him strip; has he no diseases about him?

MUSTAPHA
He is the best piece of man's flesh in the market, not an eye-sore in his whole body. Feel his legs, master; neither splint, spavin, nor wind-gall.

[Claps him on the Shoulder.

2ND MERCHANT [Feeling about him, and then putting his Hand on his Side.]
Out upon him, how his flank heaves! The whore-son is broken-winded.

MUSTAPHA
Thick-breathed a little; nothing but a sorry cold with lying out a-nights in trenches; but sound, wind and limb, I warrant him.—Try him at a loose trot a little.

[Puts the Bridle into his Hand, he strokes him.

ANTONIO
For heaven's sake, owner, spare me: you know I am but new broken.

2ND MERCHANT
'Tis but a washy jade, I see: what do you ask for this bauble?

MUSTAPHA
Bauble, do you call him? he is a substantial true-bred beast; bravely forehanded. Mark but the cleanness of his shapes too: his dam may be a Spanish gennet, but a true barb by the sire, or I have no skill in horseflesh:—Marry, I ask six hundred xeriffs for him.

[Enter **MUFTI**.

MUFTI
What is that you are asking, sirrah?

MUSTAPHA
Marry, I ask your reverence six hundred pardons; I was doing you a small piece of service here, putting off your cattle for you.

MUFTI
And putting the money into your own pocket.

MUSTAPHA
Upon vulgar reputation, no, my lord; it was for your profit and emolument. What! wrong the head of my religion? I was sensible you would have damned me, or any man, that should have injured you in a single farthing; for I knew that was sacrifice.

MUFTI

Sacrilege, you mean, sirrah,—and damning shall be the least part of your punishment: I have taken you in the manner, and will have the law upon you.

MUSTAPHA
Good my lord, take pity upon a poor man in this world, and damn me in the next.

MUFTI
No, sirrah, so you may repent and escape punishment: Did not you sell this very slave amongst the rest to me, and take money for him?

MUSTAPHA
Right, my lord.

MUFTI
And selling him again? take money twice for the same commodity? Oh, villain! but did you not know him to be my slave, sirrah?

MUSTAPHA
Why should I lie to your honour? I did know him; and thereupon, seeing him wander about, took him up for a stray, and impounded him, with intention to restore him to the right owner.

MUFTI
And yet at the same time was selling him to another: How rarely the story hangs together!

MUSTAPHA
Patience, my lord. I took him up, as your herriot, with intention to have made the best of him, and then have brought the whole product of him in a purse to you; for I know you would have spent half of it upon your pious pleasures, have hoarded up the other half, and given the remainder in charities to the poor.

MUFTI
And what's become of my other slave? Thou hast sold him too, I have a villainous suspicion.

MUSTAPHA
I know you have, my lord; but while I was managing this young robustious fellow, that old spark, who was nothing but skin and bone, and by consequence very nimble, slipt through my fingers like an eel, for there was no hold-fast of him, and ran away to buy himself a new master.

MUFTI [To **ANTONIO**.]
Follow me home, sirrah:—[To **MUSTAPHA**] I shall remember you some other time.

[Exit **MUFTI** with **ANTONIO**.

MUSTAPHA
I never doubted your lordship's memory for an ill turn: And I shall remember him too in the next rising of the mobile for this act of resumption; and more especially for the ghostly counsel he gave me before the emperor, to have hanged myself in silence to have saved his reverence. The best on't is, I am beforehand with him for selling one of his slaves twice over; and if he had not come just in the nick, I

might have pocketed up the other; for what should a poor man do that gets his living by hard labour, but pray for bad times when he may get it easily? O for some incomparable tumult! Then should I naturally wish that the beaten party might prevail; because we have plundered the other side already, and there is nothing more to get of them.

Both rich and poor for their own interest pray,
'Tis ours to make our fortune while we may;
For kingdoms are not conquered every day.

[Exit.

ACT II

SCENE I—Supposed to be a Terrace Walk, on the Side of the Castle of Alcazar

Enter **EMPEROR** and **BENDUCAR**.

EMPEROR
And thinkst thou not, it was discovered?

BENDUCAR
No:
The thoughts of kings are like religious groves,
The walks of muffled gods: Sacred retreat,
Where none, but whom they please to admit, approach.

EMPEROR
Did not my conscious eye flash out a flame,
To lighten those brown horrors, and disclose
The secret path I trod?

BENDUCAR
I could not find it, till you lent a clue
To that close labyrinth; how then should they?

EMPEROR
I would be loth they should: it breeds contempt
For herds to listen, or presume to pry,
When the hurt lion groans within his den:
But is't not strange?

BENDUCAR
To love? not more than 'tis to live; a tax
Imposed on all by nature, paid in kind,
Familiar as our being.

EMPEROR

Still 'tis strange
To me: I know my soul as wild as winds,
That sweep the desarts of our moving plains;
Love might as well be sowed upon our sands,
As in a breast so barren.
To love an enemy, the only one
Remaining too, whom yester sun beheld
Mustering her charms, and rolling, as she past
By every squadron, her alluring eyes,
To edge her champions' swords, and urge my ruin.
The shouts of soldiers, and the burst of cannon,
Maintain even still a deaf and murmuring noise;
Nor is heaven yet recovered of the sound,
Her battle roused: Yet, spite of me, I love.

BENDUCAR
What then controuls you?
Her person is as prostrate as her party.

EMPEROR
A thousand things controul this conqueror:
My native pride to own the unworthy passion,
Hazard of interest, and my people's love.
To what a storm of fate am I exposed!—
What if I had her murdered!—'tis but what
My subjects all expect, and she deserves,—
Would not the impossibility
Of ever, ever seeing, or possessing,
Calm all this rage, this hurricane of soul?

BENDUCAR
That ever, ever,—
I marked the double,—shows extreme reluctance
To part with her for ever.

EMPEROR
Right, thou hast me.
I would, but cannot kill: I must enjoy her:
I must, and what I must, be sure I will.
What's royalty, but power to please myself?
And if I dare not, then am I the slave,
And my own slaves the sovereigns:—'tis resolved.
Weak princes flatter, when they want the power
To curb their people; tender plants must bend:
But when a government is grown to strength,
Like some old oak, rough with its armed bark,
It yields not to the tug, but only nods,
And turns to sullen state.

BENDUCAR
Then you resolve
To implore her pity, and to beg relief?

EMPEROR
Death! must I beg the pity of my slave?
Must a king beg?—Yes; love's a greater king;
A tyrant, nay, a devil, that possesses me:
He tunes the organs of my voice, and speaks,
Unknown to me, within me; pushes me,
And drives me on by force.—
Say I should wed her, would not my wise subjects
Take check, and think it strange? perhaps revolt?

BENDUCAR
I hope they would not.

EMPEROR
Then thou doubtst they would?

BENDUCAR
To whom?—

EMPEROR
To her
Perhaps,—or to my brother,—or to thee.

BENDUCAR [in disorder.]
To me! me, did you mention? how I tremble!
The name of treason shakes my honest soul.
If I am doubted, sir,
Secure yourself this moment, take my life.

EMPEROR
No more: If I suspected thee—I would.

BENDUCAR
I thank your kindness.—Guilt had almost lost me. [Aside.

EMPEROR
But clear my doubts:—thinkst thou they may rebel?

BENDUCAR
This goes as I would wish.—[Aside.
'Tis possible:
A secret party still remains, that lurks
Like embers raked in ashes,—wanting but

A breath to blow aside the involving dust,
And then they blaze abroad.

EMPEROR
They must be trampled out.

BENDUCAR
But first be known.

EMPEROR
Torture shall force it from them.

BENDUCAR
You would not put a nation to the rack?

EMPEROR
Yes, the whole world; so I be safe, I care not.

BENDUCAR
Our limbs and lives
Are yours; but mixing friends with foes is hard.

EMPEROR
All may be foes; or how to be distinguished,
If some be friends?

BENDUCAR
They may with ease be winnowed.
Suppose some one, who has deserved your trust,
Some one, who knows mankind, should be employed
To mix among them, seem a malcontent,
And dive into their breasts, to try how far
They dare oppose your love?

EMPEROR
I like this well; 'tis wholesome wickedness.

BENDUCAR
Whomever he suspects, he fastens there,
And leaves no cranny of his soul unsearched;
Then like a bee bag'd with his honeyed venom,
He brings it to your hive;—if such a man,
So able and so honest, may be found;
If not, my project dies.

EMPEROR
By all my hopes, thou hast described thyself:
Thou, thou alone, art fit to play that engine,

Thou only couldst contrive.

BENDUCAR
Sure I could serve you:
I think I could:—but here's the difficulty;
I am so entirely yours,
That I should scurvily dissemble hate;
The cheat would be too gross.

EMPEROR
Art thou a statesman,
And canst not be a hypocrite? Impossible!
Do not distrust thy virtues.

BENDUCAR
If I must personate this seeming villain,
Remember 'tis to serve you.

EMPEROR
No more words:
Love goads me to Almeyda, all affairs
Are troublesome but that; and yet that most.

[Going.

Bid Dorax treat Sebastian like a king;
I had forgot him;—but this love mars all,
And takes up my whole breast.

[Exit **EMPEROR**.

BENDUCAR [To the **EMPEROR**]
Be sure I'll tell him—
With all the aggravating circumstances   [Alone.
I can, to make him swell at that command.
The tyrant first suspected me;
Then with a sudden gust he whirled about,
And trusted me too far:—Madness of power!
Now, by his own consent, I ruin him.
For, should some feeble soul, for fear or gain.
Bolt out to accuse me, even the king is cozened,
And thinks he's in the secret.
How sweet is treason, when the traitor's safe!

[Sees the **MUFTI** and **DORAX** entering, and seeming to confer.

The Mufti, and with him my sullen Dorax.
That first is mine already:

'Twas easy work to gain a covetous mind,
Whom rage to lose his prisoners had prepared:
Now caught himself,
He would seduce another. I must help him:
For churchmen, though they itch to govern all,
Are silly, woeful, aukward politicians:
They make lame mischief, though they mean it well:
Their interest is not finely drawn, and hid,
But seams are coarsely bungled up, and seen.

MUFTI
He'll tell you more.

DORAX
I have heard enough already,
To make me loath thy morals.

BENDUCAR [To **DORAX**]
You seem warm;
The good man's zeal perhaps has gone too far.

DORAX
Not very far; not farther than zeal goes;
Of course a small day's journey short of treason.

MUFTI
By all that's holy, treason was not named:
I spared the emperor's broken vows, to save
The slaves from death, though it was cheating heaven;
But I forgave him that.

DORAX
And slighted o'er
The wrongs himself sustained in property;
When his bought slaves were seized by force, no loss
Of his considered, and no cost repaid. [Scornfully.

MUFTI
Not wholly slighted o'er, not absolutely.—
Some modest hints of private wrongs I urged.

DORAX
Two-thirds of all he said: there he began
To shew the fulness of his heart; there ended.
Some short excursions of a broken vow
He made indeed, but flat insipid stuff;
But, when he made his loss the theme, he flourished,
Relieved his fainting rhetoric with new figures,

And thundered at oppressing tyranny.

MUFTI
Why not, when sacrilegious power would seize
My property? 'tis an affront to heaven,
Whose person, though unworthy, I sustain.

DORAX
You've made such strong alliances above,
That 'twere profaneness in us laity
To offer earthly aid.
I tell thee, Mufti, if the world were wise,
They would not wag one finger in your quarrels.
Your heaven you promise, but our earth you covet;
The Phætons of mankind, who fire that world,
Which you were sent by preaching but to warm.

BENDUCAR
This goes beyond the mark.

MUFTI
No, let him rail;
His prophet works within him;
He's a rare convert.

DORAX
Now his zeal yearns
To see me burned; he damns me from his church,
Because I would restrain him to his duty.—
Is not the care of souls a load sufficient?
Are not your holy stipends paid for this?
Were you not bred apart from worldly noise,
To study souls, their cures and their diseases?
If this be so, we ask you but our own:
Give us your whole employment, all your care.
The province of the soul is large enough
To fill up every cranny of your time,
And leave you much to answer, if one wretch
Be damned by your neglect.

BENDUCAR [To the **MUFTI**.]
He speaks but reason.

DORAX
Why, then, these foreign thoughts of state-employments,
Abhorrent to your function and your breedings?
Poor droning truants of unpractised cells,
Bred in the fellowship of bearded boys,

What wonder is it if you know not men?
Yet there you live demure, with down-cast eyes,
And humble as your discipline requires;
But, when let loose from thence to live at large,
Your little tincture of devotion dies:
Then luxury succeeds, and, set agog
With a new scene of yet untasted joys,
You fall with greedy hunger to the feast.
Of all your college virtues, nothing now
But your original ignorance remains;
Bloated with pride, ambition, avarice,
You swell to counsel kings, and govern kingdoms.

MUFTI
He prates as if kings had not consciences,
And none required directors but the crowd.

DORAX
As private men they want you, not as kings;
Nor would you care to inspect their public conscience,
But that it draws dependencies of power
And earthly interest, which you long to sway;
Content you with monopolizing heaven,
And let this little hanging ball alone:
For, give you but a foot of conscience there,
And you, like Archimedes, toss the globe.
We know your thoughts of us that laymen are,
Lag souls, and rubbish of remaining clay,
Which heaven, grown weary of more perfect work,
Set upright with a little puff of breath,
And bid us pass for men.

MUFTI
I will not answer,
Base foul-mouthed renegade; but I'll pray for thee,
To shew my charity.

[Exit **MUFTI**.

DORAX
Do; but forget not him who needs it most:
Allow thyself some share.—He's gone too soon;
I had to tell him of his holy jugglings;
Things that would startle faith, and make us deem
Not this, or that, but all religions false.

BENDUCAR
Our holy orator has lost the cause. [Aside.

But I shall yet redeem it.—[To **DORAX**.] Let him go;
For I have secret orders from the emperor,
Which none but you must hear: I must confess,
I could have wished some other hand had brought them.
When did you see your prisoner, great Sebastian?

DORAX
You might as well have asked me, when I saw
A crested dragon, or a basilisk;
Both are less poison to my eyes and nature,
He knows not I am I; nor shall he see me,
Till time has perfected a labouring thought,
That rolls within my breast.

BENDUCAR
'Twas my mistake.
I guessed indeed that time, and his misfortunes,
And your returning duty, had effaced
The memory of past wrongs; they would in me,
And I judged you as tame, and as forgiving.

DORAX
Forgive him! no: I left my foolish faith,
Because it would oblige me to forgiveness.

BENDUCAR
I can't but grieve to find you obstinate,
For you must see him; 'tis our emperor's will,
And strict command.

DORAX
I laugh at that command.

BENDUCAR
You must do more than see; serve, and respect him.

DORAX
See, serve him, and respect! and after all
My yet uncancelled wrongs, I must do this!—
But I forget myself.

BENDUCAR
Indeed you do.

DORAX
The emperor is a stranger to my wrongs;
I need but tell my story, to revoke
This hard commission.

BENDUCAR
Can you call me friend,
And think I could neglect to speak, at full,
The affronts you had from your ungrateful master?

DORAX
And yet enjoined my service and attendance!

BENDUCAR
And yet enjoined them both: would that were all!
He screwed his face into a hardened smile,
And said, Sebastian knew to govern slaves.

DORAX
Slaves are the growth of Africk, not of Europe.—
By heaven! I will not lay down my commission;
Not at his foot, I will not stoop so low:
But if there be a part in all his face
More sacred than the rest, I'll throw it there.

BENDUCAR
You may; but then you lose all future means
Of vengeance on Sebastian, when no more
Alcayde of this fort.

DORAX
That thought escaped me.

BENDUCAR
Keep your command, and be revenged on both:
Nor sooth yourself; you have no power to affront him;
The emperor's love protects him from insults;
And he, who spoke that proud, ill-natured word,
Following the bent of his impetuous temper,
May force your reconcilement to Sebastian;
Nay, bid you kneel, and kiss the offending foot,
That kicked you from his presence.—
But think not to divide their punishment;
You cannot touch a hair of loathed Sebastian,
While Muley-Moluch lives.

DORAX
What means this riddle?

BENDUCAR
'Tis out;—there needs no OEdipus to solve it.
Our emperor is a tyrant, feared and hated;

I scarce remember, in his reign, one day
Pass guiltless o'er his execrable head.
He thinks the sun is lost, that sees not blood:
When none is shed, we count it holiday.
We, who are most in favour, cannot call
This hour our own.—You know the younger brother,
Mild Muley-Zeydan?

DORAX
Hold, and let me think.

BENDUCAR
The soldiers idolize you;
He trusts you with the castle,
The key of all his kingdom.

DORAX
Well; and he trusts you too.

BENDUCAR
Else I were mad,
To hazard such a daring enterprize.

DORAX
He trusts us both; mark that!—Shall we betray him;
A master, who reposes life and empire
On our fidelity:—I grant he is a tyrant,
That hated name my nature most abhors:
More,—as you say,—has loaded me with scorn,
Even with the last contempt, to serve Sebastian;
Yet more, I know he vacates my revenge,
Which, but by this revolt, I cannot compass:
But, while he trusts me, 'twere so base a part,
To fawn, and yet betray,—I should be hissed,
And whooped in hell for that ingratitude.

BENDUCAR
Consider well what I have done for you.

DORAX
Consider thou, what thou wouldst have me do.

BENDUCAR
You've too much honour for a renegade.

DORAX
And thou too little faith to be a favourite.
Is not the bread thou eat'st, the robe thou wear'st,

Thy wealth, and honours, all the pure indulgence
Of him thou would'st destroy?
And would his creature, nay, his friend, betray him?
Why then no bond is left on human kind!
Distrusts, debates, immortal strifes ensue;
Children may murder parents, wives their husbands;
All must be rapine, wars, and desolation,
When trust and gratitude no longer bind.

BENDUCAR
Well have you argued in your own defence;
You, who have burst asunder all those bonds,
And turned a rebel to your native prince.

DORAX
True, I rebelled: But when did I betray?—
Indignities, which man could not support,
Provoked my vengeance to this noble crime;
But he had stripped me first of my command,
Dismissed my service, and absolved my faith;
And, with disdainful language, dared my worst:
I but accepted war, which he denounced.
Else had you seen, not Dorax, but Alonzo,
With his couched lance, against your foremost Moors;
Perhaps, too, turned the fortune of the day,
Made Africk mourn and Portugal triumph.

BENDUCAR
Let me embrace thee!

DORAX
Stand off, sycophant,
And keep infection distant.

BENDUCAR
Brave and honest!

DORAX
In spite of thy temptations.

BENDUCAR
Call them, trials;
They were no more. Thy faith was held in balance,
And nicely weighed by jealousy of power.
Vast was the trust of such a royal charge:
And our wise emperor might justly fear,
Sebastian might be freed and reconciled,
By new obligements, to thy former love.

DORAX
I doubt thee still: Thy reasons were too strong,
And driven too near the head, to be but artifice:
And, after all, I know thou art a statesman,
Where truth is rarely found.

BENDUCAR
Behold the emperor:—

[Enter **EMPEROR, SEBASTIAN,** and **ALMEYDA.**

Ask him, I beg thee,—to be justified,—
If he employed me not to ford thy soul,
And try the footing, whether false or firm.

DORAX
Death to my eyes, I see Sebastian with him!
Must he be served?—Avoid him: If we meet,
It must be like the crush of heaven and earth,
To involve us both in ruin.

[Exit.

BENDUCAR
'Twas a bare saving game I made with Dorax;
But better so than lost. He cannot hurt me;
That I precautioned: I must ruin him.—
But now this love; ay, there's the gathering storm!
The tyrant must not wed Almeyda: No!
That ruins all the fabric I am raising.
Yet, seeming to approve, it gave me time;
And gaining time gains all. [Aside.

[**BENDUCAR** goes and waits behind the **EMPEROR**.

[The **EMPEROR, SEBASTIAN,** and **ALMEYDA**, advance to the front of the stage: **GUARDS** and **ATTENDANTS**.

EMPEROR [to **SEBASTIAN**]
I bade them serve you; and, if they obey not,
I keep my lions keen within their dens,
To stop their maws with disobedient slaves.

SEBASTIAN
If I had conquered,
They could not have with more observance waited:
Their eyes, hands, feet,

Are all so quick, they seem to have but one motion,
To catch my flying words. Only the alcayde
Shuns me; and, with a grim civility,
Bows, and declines my walks.

EMPEROR
A renegade:
I know not more of him, but that he's brave,
And hates your Christian sect. If you can frame
A farther wish, give wing to your desires,
And name the thing you want.

SEBASTIAN
My liberty;
For were even paradise itself my prison,
Still I should long to leap the crystal walls.

EMPEROR
Sure our two souls have somewhere been acquainted
In former beings; or, struck out together,
One spark to Afric flew, and one to Portugal.
Expect a quick deliverance: Here's a third,

[Turning to **ALMEYDA**.

Of kindred sold to both: pity our stars
Have made us foes! I should not wish her death.

ALMEYDA
I ask no pity; if I thought my soul
Of kin to thine, soon would I rend my heart-strings,
And tear out that alliance; but thou, viper,
Hast cancelled kindred, made a rent in nature,
And through her holy bowels gnawed thy way,
Through thy own blood, to empire.

EMPEROR
This again!
And yet she lives, and only lives to upbraid me!

SEBASTIAN
What honour is there in a woman's death!
Wronged, as she says, but helpless to revenge;
Strong in her passion, impotent of reason,
Too weak to hurt, too fair to be destroyed.
Mark her majestic fabric; she's a temple
Sacred by birth, and built by hands divine;
Her souls the deity that lodges there;

Nor is the pile unworthy of the god.

EMPEROR
She's all that thou canst say, or I can think;
But the perverseness of her clamourous tongue
Strikes pity deaf.

SEBASTIAN
Then only hear her eyes!
Though they are mute, they plead; nay, more, command;
For beauteous eyes have arbitrary power.
All females have prerogative of sex;
The she's even of the savage herd are safe;
And when they snarl or bite, have no return
But courtship from the male.

EMPEROR
Were she not she, and I not Muley-Moluch,
She's mistress of inevitable charms,
For all but me; nor am I so exempt,
But that—I know not what I was to say—
But I am too obnoxious to my friends,
And swayed by your advice.

SEBASTIAN
Sir, I advised not;
By heaven, I never counselled love, but pity.

EMPEROR
By heaven thou didst; deny it not, thou didst:
For what was all that prodigality
Of praise, but to inflame me?

SEBASTIAN
Sir—

EMPEROR
No more;
Thou hast convinced me that she's worth my love.

SEBASTIAN
Was ever man so ruined by himself? [Aside.

ALMEYDA
Thy love! That odious mouth was never framed
To speak a word so soft:
Name death again, for that thou canst pronounce
With horrid grace, becoming of a tyrant.

Love is for human hearts, and not for thine,
Where the brute beast extinguishes the man.

EMPEROR
Such if I were, yet rugged lions love,
And grapple, and compel their savage dames.—
Mark my Sebastian, how that sullen frown,

[She frowns.

Like flashing lightning, opens angry heaven,
And, while it kills, delights!—But yet, insult not
Too soon, proud beauty! I confess no love.

SEBASTIAN
No, sir; I said so, and I witness for you,
Not love, but noble pity, moved your mind:
Interest might urge you too to save her life;
For those, who wish her party lost, might murmur
At shedding royal blood.

EMPEROR
Right, thou instruct'st me;
Interest of state requires not death, but marriage,
To unite the jarring titles of our line.

SEBASTIAN
Let me be dumb for ever; all I plead, [Aside.
Like wildfire thrown against the winds, returns
With double force to burn me.

EMPEROR
Could I but bend, to make my beauteous foe
The partner of my throne, and of my bed—

ALMEYDA
Still thou dissemblest; but, I read thy heart,
And know the power of my own charms; thou lov'st,
And I am pleased, for my revenge, thou dost.

EMPEROR
And thou hast cause.

ALMEYDA
I have, for I have power to make thee wretched.
Be sure I will, and yet despair of freedom.

EMPEROR

Well then, I love;
And 'tis below my greatness to disown it;
Love thee implacably, yet hate thee too;
Would hunt thee barefoot, in the mid-day sun,
Through the parched desarts and the scorching sands,
To enjoy thy love, and, once enjoyed, to kill thee.

ALMEYDA
'Tis a false courage, when thou threaten'st me;
Thou canst not stir a hand to touch my life:
Do not I see thee tremble, while thou speak'st?
Lay by the lion's hide, vain conqueror,
And take the distaff; for thy soul's my slave.

EMPEROR
Confusion! How thou view'st my very heart!
I could as soon
Stop a spring-tide, blown in, with my bare hand,
As this impetuous love:—Yes, I will wed thee;
In spite of thee, and of myself, I will.

ALMEYDA
For what? to people Africa with monsters,
Which that unnatural mixture must produce?
No, were we joined, even though it were in death,
Our bodies burning in one funeral pile,
The prodigy of Thebes would be renewed,
And my divided flame should break from thine.

EMPEROR
Serpent, I will engender poison with thee;
Join hate with hate, add venom to the birth:
Our offspring, like the seed of dragons' teeth,
Shall issue armed, and fight themselves to death.

ALMEYDA
I'm calm again; thou canst not marry me.

EMPEROR
As gleams of sunshine soften storms to showers,
So, if you smile, the loudness of my rage
In gentle whispers shall return but this—
That nothing can divert my love but death.

ALMEYDA
See how thou art deceived; I am a Christian:
'Tis true, unpractised in my new belief,
Wrongs I resent, nor pardon yet with ease;

Those fruits come late, and are of slow increase
In haughty hearts, like mine: Now, tell thyself
If this one word destroy not thy designs:
Thy law permits thee not to marry me.

EMPEROR
'Tis but a specious tale, to blast my hopes,
And baffle my pretensions.—Speak, Sebastian,
And, as a king, speak true.

SEBASTIAN
Then, thus adjured,
On a king's word 'tis truth, but truth ill-timed;
For her dear life is now exposed anew,
Unless you wholly can put on divinity,
And graciously forgive.

ALMEYDA
Now learn, by this,
The little value I have left for life,
And trouble me no more.

EMPEROR
I thank thee, woman;
Thou hast restored me to my native rage,
And I will seize my happiness by force.

SEBASTIAN
Know, Muley Moluch, when thou darest attempt—

EMPEROR
Beware! I would not be provoked to use
A conqueror's right, and therefore charge thy silence.
If thou wouldst merit to be thought my friend,
I leave thee to persuade her to compliance:
If not, there's a new gust in ravishment,
Which I have never tried.

BENDUCAR
They must be watched; [Aside.
For something I observed creates a doubt.

[Exeunt **EMPEROR** and **BENDUCAR**.

SEBASTIAN
I've been too tame, have basely borne my wrongs,
And not exerted all the king within me:
I heard him, O sweet heavens! he threatened rape;

Nay, insolently urged me to persuade thee,
Even thee, thou idol of my soul and eyes,
For whom I suffer life, and drag this being.

ALMEYDA
You turn my prison to a paradise;
But I have turned your empire to a prison:
In all your wars good fortune flew before you;
Sublime you sat in triumph on her wheel,
Till in my fatal cause your sword was drawn;
The weight of my misfortunes dragged you down.

SEBASTIAN
And is't not strange, that heaven should bless my arms
In common causes, and desert the best?
Now in your greatest, last extremity,
When I would aid you most, and most desire it,
I bring but sighs, the succours of a slave.

ALMEYDA
Leave then the luggage of your fate behind;
To make your flight more easy leave Almeyda:
Nor think me left a base, ignoble prey,
Exposed to this inhuman tyrant's lust;
My virtue is a guard beyond my strength,
And death, my last defence, within my call.

SEBASTIAN
Death may be called in vain, and cannot come;
Tyrants can tie him up from your relief;
Nor has a Christian privilege to die.
Alas, thou art too young in thy new faith:
Brutus and Cato might discharge their souls,
And give them furloughs for another world;
But we, like sentries, are obliged to stand
In starless nights, and wait the appointed hour[2].

ALMEYDA
If shunning ill be good
To those, who cannot shun it but by death,
Divines but peep on undiscovered worlds,
And draw the distant landscape as they please;
But who has e'er returned from those bright regions,
To tell their manners, and relate their laws?
I'll venture landing on that happy shore
With an unsullied body and white mind;
If I have erred, some kind inhabitant
Will pity a strayed soul, and take me home.

SEBASTIAN
Beware of death! thou canst not die unperjured,
And leave an unaccomplished love behind.
Thy vows are mine; nor will I quit my claim:
The ties of minds are but imperfect bonds,
Unless the bodies join to seal the contract.

ALMEYDA
What joys can you possess, or can I give,
Where groans of death succeed the sighs of love?
Our Hymen has not on his saffron robe;
But, muffled up in mourning, downward holds
His drooping torch, extinguished with his tears.

SEBASTIAN
The God of Love stands ready to revive it,
With his etherial breath.

ALMEYDA
'Tis late to join, when we must part so soon.

SEBASTIAN
Nay, rather let us haste it, ere we part;
Our souls, for want of that acquaintance here,
May wander in the starry walks above,
And, forced on worse companions, miss ourselves.

ALMEYDA
The tyrant will not long be absent hence;
And soon I shall be ravished from your arms.

SEBASTIAN
Wilt thou thyself become the greater tyrant,
And give not love, while thou hast love to give?
In dangerous days, when riches are a crime,
The wise betimes make over their estates:
Make o'er thy honour, by a deed of trust,
And give me seizure of the mighty wealth.

ALMEYDA
What shall I do? O teach me to refuse!
I would,—and yet I tremble at the grant;
For dire presages fright my soul by day,
And boding visions haunt my nightly dreams;
Sometimes, methinks, I hear the groans of ghosts,
Thin, hollow sounds, and lamentable screams;
Then, like a dying echo, from afar,

My mother's voice, that cries,—Wed not, Almeyda!
Forewarned, Almeyda, marriage is thy crime.

SEBASTIAN
Some envious demon to delude our joys;
Love is not sin, but where 'tis sinful love.

ALMEYDA
Mine is a flame so holy and so clear,
That the white taper leaves no soot behind;
No smoke of lust; but chaste as sisters' love,
When coldly they return a brother's kiss,
Without the zeal that meets at lovers' mouths[3].

SEBASTIAN
Laugh then at fond presages. I had some;—
Famed Nostradamus, when he took my horoscope,
Foretold my father, I should wed with incest.
Ere this unhappy war my mother died,
And sisters I had none;—vain augury!
A long religious life, a holy age,
My stars assigned me too;—impossible!
For how can incest suit with holiness,
Or priestly orders with a princely state?

ALMEYDA
Old venerable Alvarez—[Sighing.

SEBASTIAN
But why that sigh in naming that good man?

ALMEYDA
Your father's counsellor and confident—

SEBASTIAN
He was; and, if he lives, my second father.

ALMEYDA
Marked our farewell, when, going to the fight,
You gave Almeyda for the word of battle.
'Twas in that fatal moment, he discovered
The love, that long we laboured to conceal.
I know it; though my eyes stood full of tears,
Yet through the mist I saw him stedfast gaze;
Then knocked his aged breast, and inward groaned,
Like some sad prophet, that foresaw the doom
Of those whom best he loved, and could not save.

SEBASTIAN
It startles me! and brings to my remembrance,
That, when the shock of battle was begun,
He would have much complained (but had not time)
Of our hid passion: then, with lifted hands,
He begged me, by my father's sacred soul,
Not to espouse you, if he died in fight;
For, if he lived, and we were conquerors,
He had such things to urge against our marriage,
As, now declared, would blunt my sword in battle,
And dastardize my courage.

ALMEYDA
My blood curdles,
And cakes about my heart.

SEBASTIAN
I'll breathe a sigh so warm into thy bosom,
Shall make it flow again. My love, he knows not
Thou art a Christian: that produced his fear,
Lest thou shouldst sooth my soul with charms so strong,
That heaven might prove too weak.

ALMEYDA
There must be more:
This could not blunt your sword.

SEBASTIAN
Yes, if I drew it, with a curst intent,
To take a misbeliever to my bed:
It must be so.

ALMEYDA
Yet—

SEBASTIAN
No, thou shalt not plead,
With that fair mouth, against the cause of love.
Within this castle is a captive priest,
My holy confessor, whose free access
Not even the barbarous victors have refused;
This hour his hands shall make us one.

ALMEYDA
I go, with love and fortune, two blind guides,
To lead my way, half loth, and half consenting.
If, as my soul forebodes, some dire event
Pursue this union, or some crime unknown,

Forgive me, heaven! and, all ye blest above,
Excuse the frailty of unbounded love!

[Exeunt.

SCENE II—Supposed a Garden, with Lodging Rooms Behind it, or on the Sides

Enter **MUFTI, ANTONIO** as a slave, and **JOHAYMA** the MUFTI'S wife.

MUFTI
And how do you like him? look upon him well; he is a personable fellow of a Christian dog. Now, I think you are fitted for a gardener. Ha, what sayest thou, Johayma?

JOHAYMA
He may make a shift to sow lettuce, raise melons, and water a garden-plat; but otherwise, a very filthy fellow: how odiously he smells of his country garlick! fugh, how he stinks of Spain.

MUFTI
Why honey bird, I bought him on purpose for thee: didst thou not say, thou longedst for a Christian slave?

JOHAYMA
Ay, but the sight of that loathsome creature has almost cured me; and how can I tell that he is a christian? an he were well searched, he may prove a Jew, for aught I know. And, besides, I have always longed for an eunuch; for they say that's a civil creature, and almost as harmless as yourself, husband.— Speak, fellow, are not you such a kind of peaceable thing?

ANTONIO
I was never taken for one in my own country; and not very peaceable neither, when I am well provoked.

MUFTI
To your occupation, dog; bind up the jessamines in yonder arbour, and handle your pruning-knife with dexterity: tightly I say, go tightly to your business; you have cost me much, and must earn it in your work. Here's plentiful provision for you, rascal; salading in the garden, and water in the tank, and on holidays the licking of a platter of rice, when you deserve it.

JOHAYMA
What have you been bred up to, sirrah? and what can you perform, to recommend you to my service?

ANTONIO [Making Legs.]
Why, madam, I can perform as much as any man, in a fair lady's service. I can play upon the flute, and sing; I can carry your umbrella, and fan your ladyship, and cool you when you are too hot; in fine, no service, either by day or by night, shall come amiss to me; and, besides I am of so quick an apprehension, that you need but wink upon me at any time to make me understand my duty.

[She winks at him.]

—Very fine, she has tipt the wink already. [Aside.

JOHAYMA
The whelp may come to something in time, when I have entered him into his business.

MUFTI
A very malapert cur, I can tell him that; I do not like his fawning—You must be taught your distance, sirrah.

[Strikes him.

JOHAYMA
Hold, hold. He has deserved it, I confess; but, for once, let his ignorance plead his pardon; we must not discourage a beginner. Your reverence has taught us charity, even to birds and beasts:—here, you filthy brute, you, take this little alms to buy you plasters.

[Gives him a piece of money.

ANTONIO
Money, and a love-pinch in the inside of my palm into the bargain. [Aside.

[Enter a **SERVANT**.

SERVANT
Sir, my lord Benducar is coming to wait on you, and is already at the palace gate.

MUFTI
Come in, Johayma; regulate the rest of my wives and concubines, and leave the fellow to his work.

JOHAYMA
How stupidly he stares about him, like a calf new come into the world! I shall teach you, sirrah, to know your business a little better. This way, you awkward rascal; here lies the arbour; must I be shewing you eternally?

[Turning him about.

MUFTI
Come away, minion; you shall shew him nothing.

JOHAYMA
I'll but bring him into the arbour, where a rose-tree and a myrtle-tree are just falling for want of a prop; if they were bound together, they would help to keep up one another. He's a raw gardener, and 'tis but charity to teach him.

MUFTI
No more deeds of charity to-day; come in, or I shall think you a little better disposed than I could wish you.

JOHAYMA
Well, go before, I will follow my pastor.

MUFTI
So you may cast a sheep's eye behind you? in before me;—and you, sauciness, mind your pruning-knife, or I may chance to use it for you.

[Exeunt **MUFTI** and **JOHAYMA**.

ANTONIO [Alone.]
Thank you for that, but I am in no such haste to be made a mussulman. For his wedlock, for all her haughtiness, I find her coming. How far a Christian should resist, I partly know; but how far a lewd young Christian can resist, is another question. She's tolerable, and I am a poor stranger, far from better friends, and in a bodily necessity. Now have I a strange temptation to try what other females are belonging to this family: I am not far from the women's apartment, I am sure; and if these birds are within distance, here's that will chuckle them together.

[Pulls out his Flute.]

If there be variety of Moors' flesh in this holy market, 'twere madness to lay out all my money upon the first bargain.

[He plays. A Grate opens, and **MORAYMA**, the Mufti's Daughter, appears at it.]

—Ay, there's an apparition! This is a morsel worthy of a Mufti; this is the relishing bit in secret; this is the mystery of his Alcoran, that must be reserved from the knowledge of the prophane vulgar; this is his holiday devotion.—See, she beckons too.

[She beckons to him.

MORAYMA
Come a little nearer, and speak softly.

ANTONIO
I come. I come, I warrant thee; the least twinkle had brought me to thee; such another kind syllable or two would turn me to a meteor, and draw me up to thee.

MORAYMA
I dare not speak, for fear of being overheard; but if you think my person worth your hazard, and can deserve my love, the rest this note shall tell you.

[Throws down a Handkerchief.]

No more, my heart goes with you.

[Exit from the Grate.

ANTONIO
O thou pretty little heart, art thou flown hither? I'll keep it warm, I warrant it, and brood upon it in the new nest.—But now for my treasure trove, that's wrapt up in the handkerchief; no peeping here, though I long to be spelling her Arabic scrawls and pot-hooks. But I must carry off my prize as robbers do, and not think of sharing the booty before I am free from danger, and out of eye-shot from the other windows. If her wit be as poignant as her eyes, I am a double slave. Our northern beauties are mere dough to these; insipid white earth, mere tobacco pipe clay, with no more soul and motion in them than a fly in winter.
Here the warm planet ripens and sublimes
The well-baked beauties of the southern climes.
Our Cupid's but a bungler in his trade;
His keenest arrows are in Africk made.

[Exit.

ACT III

SCENE I—A Terrace Walk; or some other public place in the castle of Alcazar

Enter **EMPEROR, MULEY-MOLUCH**, and **BENDUCAR**.

EMPEROR
Married! I'll not believe it; 'tis imposture;
Improbable they should presume to attempt,
Impossible they should effect their wish.

BENDUCAR
Have patience, till I clear it.

EMPEROR
I have none:
Go bid our moving plains of sand lie still,
And stir not, when the stormy south blows high:
From top to bottom thou hast tossed my soul,
And now 'tis in the madness of the whirl,
Requir'st a sudden stop? unsay thy lie;
That may in time do somewhat.

BENDUCAR
I have done:
For, since it pleases you it should be forged,
'Tis fit it should: far be it from your slave
To raise disturbance in your sacred breast.

EMPEROR
Sebastian is my slave as well as thou;

Nor durst offend my love by that presumption.

BENDUCAR
Most sure he ought not.

EMPEROR
Then all means were wanting:
No priest, no ceremonies of their sect;
Or, grant we these defects could be supplied,
How could our prophet do an act so base,
So to resume his gifts, and curse my conquests,
By making me unhappy? No, the slave,
That told thee so absurd a story, lied.

BENDUCAR
Yet till this moment I have found him faithful:
He said he saw it too.

EMPEROR
Dispatch; what saw he?

BENDUCAR
Truth is, considering with what earnestness
Sebastian pleaded for Almeyda's life,
Enhanced her beauty, dwelt upon her praise—

EMPEROR
O stupid, and unthinking as I was!
I might have marked it too; 'twas gross and palpable.

BENDUCAR
Methought I traced a lover ill disguised,
And sent my spy, a sharp observing slave,
To inform me better, if I guessed aright.
He told me, that he saw Sebastian's page
Run cross the marble square, who soon returned,
And after him there lagged a puffing friar;
Close wrapt he bore some secret instrument
Of Christian superstition in his hand:
My servant followed fast, and through a chink
Perceived the royal captives hand in hand;
And heard the hooded father mumbling charms,
That make those misbelievers man and wife;
Which done, the spouses kissed with such a fervour,
And gave such furious earnest of their flames,
That their eyes sparkled, and their mantling blood
Flew flushing o'er their faces.

EMPEROR
Hell confound them!

BENDUCAR
The reverend father, with a holy leer,
Saw he might well be spared, and soon withdrew:
This forced my servant to a quick retreat,
For fear to be discovered.—Guess the rest.

EMPEROR
I do: My fancy is too exquisite,
And tortures me with their imagined bliss.
Some earthquake should have risen and rent the ground,
Have swallowed him, and left the longing bride
In agony of unaccomplished love.

[Walks disorderly.

[Enter the **MUFTI**.

BENDUCAR
In an unlucky hour
That fool intrudes, raw in this great affair,
And uninstructed how to stem the tide.—[Aside.

[Coming up the **MUFTI**,—aside.]

The emperor must not marry, nor enjoy:—
Keep to that point: Stand firm, for all's at stake.

EMPEROR [Seeing him.]
You druggerman[4] of heaven, must I attend
Your droning prayers? Why came ye not before?
Dost thou not know the captive king has dared
To wed Almeyda? Cancel me that marriage,
And make her mine: About the business, quick!—
Expound thy Mahomet; make him speak my sense,
Or he's no prophet here, and thou no Mufti;
Unless thou know'st the trick of thy vocation,
To wrest and rend the law, to please thy prince.

MUFTI
Why, verily, the law is monstrous plain:
There's not one doubtful text in all the alcoran,
Which can be wrenched in favour to your project.

EMPEROR
Forge one, and foist it into some bye-place

Of some old rotten roll: Do't, I command thee!
Must I teach thee thy trade?

MUFTI
It cannot be;
For matrimony being the dearest point
Of law, the people have it all by heart:
A cheat on procreation will not pass.
Besides, [In a higher tone.] the offence is so exorbitant,
To mingle with a misbelieving race,
That speedy vengeance would pursue your crime,
And holy Mahomet launch himself from heaven,
Before the unready thunderbolts were formed.

[**EMPEROR**, taking him by the throat with one hand, snatches out his sword with the other, and points it to his breast.

EMPEROR
Slave, have I raised thee to this pomp and power,
To preach against my will?—Know, I am law;
And thou, not Mahomet's messenger but mine!—
Make it, I charge thee, make my pleasure lawful;
Or, first, I strip thee of thy ghostly greatness,
Then send thee post to tell thy tale above.
And bring thy vain memorials to thy prophet,
Of justice done below for disobedience.

MUFTI
For heaven's sake hold!—The respite of a moment!—
To think for you—

EMPEROR
And for thyself.

MUFTI
For both.

BENDUCAR
Disgrace, and death, and avarice, have lost him! [Aside.

MUFTI
'Tis true, our law forbids to wed a Christian;
But it forbids you not to ravish her.
You have a conqueror's right upon your slave;
And then the more despite you do a Christian,
You serve the prophet more, who loathes that sect.

EMPEROR

O, now it mends; and you talk reason, Mufti.—
But, stay! I promised freedom to Sebastian;
Now, should I grant it, his revengeful soul
Would ne'er forgive his violated bed.

MUFTI
Kill him; for then you give him liberty:
His soul is from his earthly prison freed.

EMPEROR
How happy is the prince who has a churchman,
So learned and pliant, to expound his laws!

BENDUCAR
Two things I humbly offer to your prudence.

EMPEROR
Be brief, but let not either thwart my love.

BENDUCAR
First, since our holy man has made rape lawful,
Fright her with that; Proceed not yet to force:
Why should you pluck the green distasteful fruit
From the unwilling bough,
When it may ripen of itself, and fall?

EMPEROR
Grant her a day; though that's too much to give
Out of a life which I devote to love.

BENDUCAR
Then, next, to bar
All future hopes of her desired Sebastian,
Let Dorax be enjoined to bring his head.

EMPEROR [To the **MUFTI**]
Go, Mufti, call him to receive his orders.—

[Exit **MUFTI**.

I taste thy counsel; her desires new roused,
And yet unslaked, will kindle in her fancy,
And make her eager to renew the feast.

BENDUCAR [Aside.]
Dorax, I know before, will disobey:
There's a foe's head well cropped.—
But this hot love precipitates my plot,

And brings it to projection ere its time.

[Enter **SEBASTIAN** and **ALMEYDA**, hand in hand; upon sight of the **EMPEROR**, they separate, and seem disturbed.

ALMEYDA
He breaks at unawares upon our walks,
And, like a midnight wolf, invades the fold.
Make speedy preparation of your soul,
And bid it arm apace: He comes for answer,
And brutal mischief sits upon his brow.

SEBASTIAN
Not the last sounding could surprise me more,
That summons drowsy mortals to their doom,
When called in haste to fumble for their limbs,
And tremble, unprovided for their charge:
My sense has been so deeply plunged in joys,
The soul out-slept her hour; and, scarce awake,
Would think too late, but cannot: But brave minds,
At worst, can dare their fate. [Aside.

EMPEROR [Coming up to them.]
Have you performed
Your embassy, and treated with success?

SEBASTIAN
I had no time.

EMPEROR
No, not for my affairs;
But, for your own, too much.

SEBASTIAN
You talk in clouds; explain your meaning, sir.

EMPEROR
Explain yours first.—What meant you, hand in hand?
And, when you saw me, with a guilty start,
You loosed your hold, affrighted at my presence.

SEBASTIAN
Affrighted!

EMPEROR
Yes, astonished and confounded.

SEBASTIAN

What mak'st thou of thyself, and what of me?
Art thou some ghost, some demon, or some god,
That I should stand astonished at thy sight?
If thou could'st deem so meanly of my courage,
Why didst thou not engage me man for man,
And try the virtue of that Gorgon face,
To stare me into statue?

EMPEROR
Oh, thou art now recovered; but, by heaven,
Thou wert amazed at first, as if surprised
At unexpected baseness brought to light.
For know, ungrateful man, that kings, like gods,
Are every where; walk in the abyss of minds,
And view the dark recesses of the soul.

SEBASTIAN
Base and ungrateful never was I thought;
Nor, till this turn of fate, durst thou have called me:
But, since thou boast'st the omniscience of a god,
Say in what cranny of Sebastian's soul,
Unknown to me, so loathed a crime is lodged?

EMPEROR
Thou hast not broke my trust, reposed in thee!

SEBASTIAN
Imposed, but not received.—Take back that falsehood.

EMPEROR
Thou art not married to Almeyda?

SEBASTIAN
Yes.

EMPEROR
And own'st the usurpation of my love?

SEBASTIAN
I own it, in the face of heaven and thee;
No usurpation, but a lawful claim,
Of which I stand possessed.

EMPEROR
She has chosen well,
Betwixt a captive and a conqueror.

ALMEYDA

Betwixt a monster, and the best of men!—
He was the envy of his neighbouring kings;
For him their sighing queens despised their lords;
And virgin daughters blushed when he was named.
To share his noble chains is more to me,
Than all the savage greatness of thy throne.

SEBASTIAN
Were I to chuse again, and knew my fate,
For such a night I would be what I am.
The joys I have possessed are ever mine;
Out of thy reach; behind eternity;
Hid in the sacred treasure of the past:
But blest remembrance brings them hourly back.

EMPEROR
Hourly indeed, who hast but hours to live.
O, mighty purchase of a boasted bliss!
To dream of what thou hadst one fugitive night,
And never shalt have more!

SEBASTIAN
Barbarian, thou canst part us but a moment!
We shall be one again in thy despite.
Life is but air,
That yields a passage to the whistling sword,
And closes when 'tis gone.

ALMEYDA
How can we better die than close embraced,
Sucking each other's souls while we expire?
Which, so transfused, and mounting both at once,
The saints, deceived, shall, by a sweet mistake,
Hand up thy soul for mine, and mine for thine.

EMPEROR
No, I'll untwist you:
I have occasion for your stay on earth.
Let him mount first, and beat upon the wing,
And wait an age for what I here detain;
Or sicken at immortal joys above,
And languish for the heaven he left below.

ALMEYDA
Thou wilt not dare to break what heaven has joined?

EMPEROR
Not break the chain; but change a rotten link,

And rivet one to last.
Think'st thou I come to argue right and wrong?—
Why lingers Dorax thus? Where are my guards,

[**BENDUCAR** goes out for the **GUARDS**, and returns.

To drag that slave to death?—

[Pointing to **SEBASTIAN**.

Now storm and rage;
Call vainly on thy prophet, then defy him
For wanting power to save thee.

SEBASTIAN
That were to gratify thy pride. I'll shew thee
How a man should, and how a king dare die!
So even, that my soul shall walk with ease
Out of its flesh, and shut out life as calmly
As it does words; without a sign to note
One struggle, in the smooth dissolving frame.

ALMEYDA [To the **EMPEROR**]
Expect revenge from heaven, inhuman wretch!
Nor hope to ascend Sebastian's holy bed.
Flames, daggers, poisons, guard the sacred steps:
Those are the promised pleasures of my love.

EMPEROR
And these might fright another, but not me;
Or me, if I designed to give you pleasure.
I seek my own; and while that lasts, you live.—

[Enter two of the **GUARDS**.

Go, bear the captive to a speedy death,
And set my soul at ease.

ALMEYDA
I charge you hold, ye ministers of death!—
Speak my Sebastian;
Plead for thy life; Oh, ask it of the tyrant:
'Tis no dishonour; trust me, love, 'tis none.
I would die for thee, but I cannot plead;
My haughty heart disdains it, even for thee.—
Still silent! Will the king of Portugal
Go to his death like a dumb sacrifice?
Beg him to save my life in saving thine.

SEBASTIAN
Farewell; my life's not worth another word.

EMPEROR [To the **GUARDS**]
Perform your orders.

ALMEYDA
Stay, take my farewell too!
Farewell the greatness of Almeyda's soul!—
Look, tyrant, what excess of love can do;
It pulls me down thus low as to thy feet;

[Kneels to him.

Nay, to embrace thy knees with loathing hands,
Which blister when they touch thee: Yet even thus,
Thus far I can, to save Sebastian's life.

EMPEROR
A secret pleasure trickles through my veins:
It works about the inlets of my soul,
To feel thy touch, and pity tempts the pass:
But the tough metal of my heart resists;
'Tis warmed with the soft fire, not melted down.

ALMEYDA
A flood of scalding tears will make it run.
Spare him, Oh spare! Can you pretend to love,
And have no pity? Love and that are twins.
Here will I grow;
Thus compass you with these supplanting cords,
And pull so long till the proud fabrick falls.

EMPEROR
Still kneel, and still embrace: 'Tis double pleasure,
So to be hugged, and see Sebastian die.

ALMEYDA
Look, tyrant, when thou nam'st Sebastian's death,
Thy very executioners turn pale.
Rough as they are, and hardened in their trade
Of death, they start at an anointed head,
And tremble to approach.—He hears me not,
Nor minds the impression of a god on kings;
Because no stamp of heaven was on his soul,
But the resisting mass drove back the seal.—
Say, though thy heart be rock of adamant,

Yet rocks are not impregnable to bribes:
Instruct me how to bribe thee; name thy price;
Lo, I resign my title to the crown;
Send me to exile with the man I love,
And banishment is empire.

EMPEROR
Here's my claim,

[Clapping his Hand to his Sword.

And this extinguished thine; thou giv'st me nothing.

ALMEYDA
My father's, mother's, brother's death, I pardon;
That's somewhat sure; a mighty sum of murder,
Of innocent and kindred blood struck off.
My prayers and penance shall discount for these,
And beg of heaven to charge the bill on me:
Behold what price I offer, and how dear,
To buy Sebastian's life!

EMPEROR
Let after-reckonings trouble fearful fools;
I'll stand the trial of those trivial crimes:
But, since thou begg'st me to prescribe my terms,
The only I can offer are thy love,
And this one day of respite to resolve.
Grant, or deny; for thy next word is fate,
And fate is deaf to prayer.

ALMEYDA
May heaven be so,

[Rising up.

At thy last breath, to thine! I curse thee not;
For, who can better curse the plague, or devil,
Than to be what they are? That curse be thine.—
Now, do not speak, Sebastian, for you need not;
But die, for I resign your life.—Look, heaven,
Almeyda dooms her dear Sebastian's death!
But is there heaven? for I begin to doubt;
The skies are hushed, no grumbling thunders roll.—
Now take your swing, ye impious; sin unpunished;
Eternal Providence seems overwatched,
And with a slumbering nod assents to murder.

[Enter **DORAX**, attended by three **SOLDIERS**.

EMPEROR
Thou mov'st a tortoise-pace to my relief.
Take hence that once a king; that sullen pride,
That swells to dumbness: lay him in the dungeon,
And sink him deep with irons, that, when he would,
He shall not groan to hearing; when I send,
The next commands are death.

ALMEYDA
Then prayers are vain as curses.

EMPEROR
Much at one
In a slave's mouth, against a monarch's power.
This day thou hast to think;
At night, if thou wilt curse, thou shalt curse kindly;
Then I'll provoke thy lips, lay siege so close,
That all thy sallying breath shall turn to blessings.—
Make haste, seize, force her, bear her hence.

ALMEYDA
Farewell, my last Sebastian!
I do not beg, I challenge justice now.—
O Powers, if kings be your peculiar care,
Why plays this wretch with your prerogative?
Now flash him dead, now crumble him to ashes,
Or henceforth live confined in your own palace;
And look not idly out upon a world,
That is no longer yours.

[She is carried off struggling; **EMPEROR** and **BENDUCAR** follow. **SEBASTIAN** struggles in his **GUARD'S** arms, and shakes off one of them; but two others come in, and hold him; he speaks not all the while.

DORAX
I find I'm but a half-strained villain yet;
But mongrel-mischievous; for my blood boiled,
To view this brutal act; and my stern soul
Tugged at my arm, to draw in her defence. [Aside.
Down, thou rebelling Christian in my heart!
Redeem thy fame on this Sebastian first;

[Walks a turn.

Then think on other wrongs, when thine are righted.
But how to right them? on a slave disarmed,
Defenceless, and submitted to my rage?

A base revenge is vengeance on myself:—

[Walks again.

I have it, and I thank thee, honest head,
Thus present to me at my great necessity.—

[Comes up to **SEBASTIAN**.

You know me not?

SEBASTIAN
I hear men call thee Dorax.

DORAX
'Tis well; you know enough for once:—you speak too;
You were struck mute before.

SEBASTIAN
Silence became me then.

DORAX
Yet we may talk hereafter.

SEBASTIAN
Hereafter is not mine:
Dispatch thy work, good executioner.

DORAX
None of my blood were hangmen; add that falsehood
To a long bill, that yet remains unreckoned.

SEBASTIAN
A king and thou can never have a reckoning.

DORAX
A greater sum, perhaps, than you can pay.
Meantime, I shall make bold to increase your debt;

[Gives him his Sword.

Take this, and use it at your greatest need.

SEBASTIAN
This hand and this have been acquainted well:

[Looks on it.

It should have come before into my grasp,
To kill the ravisher.

DORAX
Thou heard'st the tyrant's orders; guard thy life
When 'tis attacked, and guard it like a man.

SEBASTIAN
I'm still without thy meaning, but I thank thee.

DORAX
Thank me when I ask thanks; thank me with that.

SEBASTIAN
Such surly kindness did I never see.

DORAX [To the **CAPTAIN** of his Guards.]
Musa, draw out a file; pick man by man.
Such who dare die, and dear will sell their death.
Guard him to the utmost; now conduct him hence,
And treat him as my person.

SEBASTIAN
Something like
That voice, methinks, I should have somewhere heard;
But floods of woes have hurried it far off,
Beyond my ken of soul.

[Exit **SEBASTIAN**, with the **SOLDIERS**.

DORAX
But I shall bring him back, ungrateful man!
I shall, and set him full before thy sight,
When I shall front thee, like some staring ghost,
With all my wrongs about me.—What, so soon
Returned? this haste is boding.

[Enter to him **EMPEROR**, **BENDUCAR**, and **MUFTI**.

EMPEROR
She's still inexorable, still imperious,
And loud, as if, like Bacchus, born in thunder.
Be quick, ye false physicians of my mind;
Bring speedy death, or cure.

BENDUCAR
What can be counselled, while Sebastian lives?
The vine will cling, while the tall poplar stands;

But, that cut down, creeps to the next support,
And twines as closely there.

EMPEROR
That's done with ease; I speak him dead:—proceed.

MUFTI
Proclaim your marriage with Almeyda next,
That civil wars may cease; this gains the crowd:
Then you may safely force her to your will;
For people side with violence and injustice,
When done for public good.

EMPEROR
Preach thou that doctrine.

BENDUCAR
The unreasonable fool has broached a truth,
That blasts my hopes; but, since 'tis gone so far,
He shall divulge Almeyda is a Christian;
If that produce no tumult, I despair. [Aside.

EMPEROR
Why speaks not Dorax?

DORAX
Because my soul abhors to mix with him.
Sir, let me bluntly say, you went too far,
To trust the preaching power on state-affairs
To him, or any heavenly demagogue:
'Tis a limb lopt from your prerogative,
And so much of heaven's image blotted from you.

MUFTI
Sure thou hast never heard of holy men,
(So Christians call them) famed in state affairs!
Such as in Spain, Ximenes, Albornoz;
In England, Wolsey; match me these with laymen.

DORAX
How you triumph in one or two of these,
Born to be statesmen, happening to be churchmen!
Thou call'st them holy; so their function was:
But tell me, Mufti, which of them were saints?—
Next sir, to you: the sum of all is this,—
Since he claims power from heaven, and not from kings,
When 'tis his interest, he can interest heaven
To preach you down; and ages oft depend

On hours, uninterrupted, in the chair.

EMPEROR
I'll trust his preaching, while I rule his pay;
And I dare trust my Africans to hear
Whatever he dare preach.

DORAX
You know them not.
The genius of your Moors is mutiny;
They scarcely want a guide to move their madness;
Prompt to rebel on every weak pretence;
Blustering when courted, crouching when opprest;
Wise to themselves, and fools to all the world;
Restless in change, and perjured to a proverb.
They love religion sweetened to the sense;
A good, luxurious, palatable faith.
Thus vice and godliness,—preposterous pair!—
Ride cheek by jowl, but churchmen hold the reins:
And whene'er kings would lower clergy-greatness,
They learn too late what power the preachers have,
And whose the subjects are; the Mufti knows it,
Nor dares deny what passed betwixt us two.

EMPEROR
No more; whate'er he said was my command.

DORAX
Why, then, no more, since you will hear no more;
Some kings are resolute to their own ruin.

EMPEROR
Without your meddling where you are not asked,
Obey your orders, and dispatch Sebastian.

DORAX
Trust my revenge; be sure I wish him dead.

EMPEROR
What mean'st thou? What's thy wishing to my will?
Dispatch him; rid me of the man I loath.

DORAX
I hear you, sir; I'll take my time, and do't.

EMPEROR
Thy time! What's all thy time? What's thy whole life
To my one hour of ease? No more replies,

But see thou dost it; or—

DORAX
Choke in that threat; I can say or as loud.

EMPEROR
'Tis well; I see my words have no effect,
But I may send a message to dispose you.

[Is going off.

DORAX
Expect an answer worthy of that message.

MUFTI
The prophet owed him this;
And, thanked be heaven, he has it. [Aside.

BENDUCAR
By holy Alla, I conjure you stay,
And judge not rashly of so brave a man.

[Draws the **EMPEROR** aside, and whispers him.

I'll give you reasons why he cannot execute
Your orders now, and why he will hereafter.

MUFTI
Benducar is a fool, to bring him off;
I'll work my own revenge, and speedily. [Aside.

BENDUCAR
The fort is his, the soldiers' hearts are his;
A thousand Christian slaves are in the castle,
Which he can free to reinforce his power;
Your troops far off, beleaguering Larache,
Yet in the Christians' hands.

EMPEROR
I grant all this;
But grant me he must die.

BENDUCAR
He shall, by poison;
'Tis here, the deadly drug, prepared in powder,
Hot as hell fire: Then, to prevent his soldiers
From rising to revenge their general's death,
While he is struggling with his mortal pangs,

The rabble on the sudden may be raised
To seize the castle.

EMPEROR
Do't;—'tis left to thee.

BENDUCAR
Yet more;—but clear your brow, for he observes.

[They whisper again.

DORAX
What, will the favourite prop my falling fortunes?
O prodigy of court! [Aside

[**EMPEROR** and **BENDUCAR** return to **DORAX**.

EMPEROR
Your friend has fully cleared your innocence;
I was too hasty to condemn unheard,
And you, perhaps, too prompt in your replies.
As far as fits the majesty of kings,
I ask excuse.

DORAX
I'm sure I meant it well.

EMPEROR
I know you did:—This to our love renewed.—

[**EMPEROR**. drinks.

Benducar, fill to Dorax.

[**BENDUCAR** turns, and mixes a Powder in it.

DORAX
Let it go round, for all of us have need
To quench our heats: 'Tis the king's health, Benducar,

[He drinks.

And I would pledge it, though I knew 'twere poison.

BENDUCAR
Another bowl; for what the king has touched,
And you have pledged, is sacred to your loves.

[Drinks out of another Bowl.

MUFTI
Since charity becomes my calling, thus
Let me provoke your friendship; and heaven bless it,
As I intend it well.

[Drinks; and, turning aside, pours some drops out of a little vial into the Bowl; then presents it to **DORAX**.

DORAX
Heaven make thee honest;
On that condition we shall soon be friends.

[Drinks.

MUFTI
Yes, at our meeting in another world;
For thou hast drunk thy passport out of this.
Not the Nonacrian font, nor Lethe's lake,
Could sooner numb thy nimble faculties,
Than this, to sleep eternal. [Aside.

EMPEROR
Now farewell, Dorax; this was our first quarrel,
And, I dare prophecy, will prove our last.

[Exeunt **EMPEROR**, **BENDUCAR** and the **MUFTI**.

DORAX
It may be so.—I'm strangely discomposed;
Quick shootings thro' my limbs, and pricking pains,
Qualms at my heart, convulsions in my nerves,
Shiverings of cold, and burnings of my entrails,
Within my little world make medley war,
Lose and regain, beat, and are beaten back,
As momentary victors quit their ground.—
Can it be poison! Poison's of one tenor,
Or hot, or cold; this neither, and yet both.
Some deadly draught, some enemy of life,
Boils in my bowels, and works out my soul.
Ingratitude's the growth of every clime;
Africk, the scene removed, is Portugal.
Of all court service, learn the common lot,—
To-day 'tis done, to-morrow 'tis forgot.
Oh, were that all! my honest corpse must lie
Exposed to scorn, and public infamy;
My shameful death will be divulged alone;

The worth and honour of my soul unknown.

[Exit.

SCENE II.—A Night-Scene of the Mufti's Garden, Where an Arbour is Discovered

Enter **ANTONIO**.

ANTONIO
She names herself Morayma; the Mufti's only daughter, and a virgin! This is the time and place that she appointed in her letter, yet she comes not. Why, thou sweet delicious creature, why torture me with thy delay! Dar'st thou be false to thy assignation? What, in the cool and silence of the night, and to a new lover?—Pox on the hypocrite, thy father, for instructing thee so little in the sweetest point of his religion.—Hark, I hear the rustling of her silk mantle. Now she comes, now she comes:—no, hang it, that was but the whistling of the wind through the orange-trees.—Now, again, I hear the pit-a-pat of a pretty foot through the dark alley:—No, 'tis the son of a mare, that's broken loose, and munching upon the melons.—Oh, the misery of an expecting lover! Well, I'll e'en despair, go into my arbour, and try to sleep; in a dream I shall enjoy her, in despite of her.

[Goes into the Arbour, and lies down.

[Enter **JOHAYMA**, wrapt up in a Moorish mantle.

JOHAYMA
Thus far my love has carried me, almost without my knowledge whither I was going. Shall I go on? shall I discover myself?—What an injury am I doing to my old husband! Yet what injury, since he's old, and has three wives, and six concubines, besides me! 'tis but stealing my own tithe from him.

[She comes a little nearer the Arbour.

ANTONIO [Raising himself a little, and looking.]
At last 'tis she; this is no illusion, I am sure; 'tis a true she-devil of flesh and blood, and she could never have taken a fitter time to tempt me.

JOHAYMA
He's young and handsome—

ANTONIO
Yes, well enough, I thank nature. [Aside.

JOHAYMA
And I am yet neither old nor ugly: Sure he will not refuse me.

ANTONIO
No; thou may'st pawn thy maidenhead upon't, he wont. [Aside.

JOHAYMA

The Mufti would feast himself upon other women, and keep me fasting.

ANTONIO
O, the holy curmudgeon! [Aside.

JOHAYMA
Would preach abstinence, and practise luxury! but, I thank my stars, I have edified more by his example than his precept.

ANTONIO [Aside.]
Most divinely argued; she's the best casuist in all Africk.

[He rushes out, and embraces her.]

I can hold no longer from embracing thee, my dear Morayma; the old unconscionable whoreson, thy father, could he expect cold chastity from a child of his begetting?

JOHAYMA
What nonsense do you talk? do you take me for the Mufti's daughter?

ANTONIO
Why, are you not, madam?

[Throwing off her barnus.

JOHAYMA
I find you had an appointment with Morayma.

ANTONIO
By all that's good, the nauseous wife! [Aside.

JOHAYMA
What! you are confounded, and stand mute?

ANTONIO
Somewhat nonplust, I confess, to hear you deny your name so positively. Why, are not you Morayma, the Mufti's daughter? Did not I see you with him: did not he present me to you? were you not so charitable as to give me money? ay, and to tread upon my foot, and squeeze my hand too, if I may be so bold to remember you of past favours?

JOHAYMA
And you see I am come to make them good; but I am neither Morayma, nor the Mufti's daughter.

ANTONIO
Nay, I know not that: but I am sure he is old enough to be your father; and either father, or reverend father, I heard you call him.

JOHAYMA

Once again, how came you to name Morayma?

ANTONIO
Another damned mistake of mine: for, asking one of my fellow-slaves, who were the chief ladies about the house, he answered me, Morayma and Johayma; but she, it seems, is his daughter, with a pox to her, and you are his beloved wife.

JOHAYMA
Say your beloved mistress, if you please; for that's the title I desire. This moonshine grows offensive to my eyes; come, shall we walk into the arbour? there we may rectify all mistakes.

ANTONIO
That's close and dark.

JOHAYMA
And are those faults to lovers?

ANTONIO
But there I cannot please myself with the sight of your beauty.

JOHAYMA
Perhaps you may do better.

ANTONIO
But there's not a breath of air stirring.

JOHAYMA
The breath of lovers is the sweetest air; but you are fearful.

ANTONIO
I am considering indeed, that, if I am taken with you—

JOHAYMA
The best way to avoid it is to retire, where we may not be discovered.

ANTONIO
Where lodges your husband?

JOHAYMA
Just against the face of this open walk.

ANTONIO
Then he has seen us already, for aught I know.

JOHAYMA
You make so many difficulties, I fear I am displeasing to you.

ANTONIO [Aside.]

If Morayma comes, and takes me in the arbour with her, I have made a fine exchange of that diamond for this pebble.

JOHAYMA
You are much fallen off, let me tell you, from the fury of your first embrace.

ANTONIO
I confess I was somewhat too furious at first, but you will forgive the transport of my passion; now I have considered it better, I have a qualm of conscience.

JOHAYMA
Of conscience! why, what has conscience to do with two young lovers that have opportunity?

ANTONIO
Why, truly, conscience is something to blame for interposing in our matters: but how can I help it, if I have a scruple to betray my master?

JOHAYMA
There must be something more in't; for your conscience was very quiet when you took me for Morayma.

ANTONIO
I grant you, madam, when I took you for his daughter; for then I might have made you an honourable amends by marriage.

JOHAYMA
You Christians are such peeking sinners! you tremble at a shadow in the moonshine.

ANTONIO
And you Africans are such termagants, you stop at nothing. I must be plain with you,—you are married, and to a holy man, the head of your religion: go back to your chamber; go back, I say, and consider of it for this night, as I will do on my part: I will be true to you, and invent all the arguments I can to comply with you; and who knows but at our next meeting the sweet devil may have more power over me? I am true flesh and blood, I can tell you that for your comfort.

JOHAYMA
Flesh without blood, I think thou art; or, if any, it is as cold as that of fishes. But I'll teach thee, to thy cost, what vengeance is in store for refusing a lady who has offered thee her love.—Help, help, there! will nobody come to my assistance?

ANTONIO
What do you mean, madam? for heaven's sake, peace; your husband will hear you; think of your own danger, if you will not think of
mine.

JOHAYMA
Ungrateful wretch, thou deservest no pity!—Help, help, husband, or I shall be ravished! the villain will be too strong for me! Help, help, for pity of a poor distressed creature!

ANTONIO
Then I have nothing but impudence to assist me: I must drown her clamour, whatever comes on't.

[He takes out his Flute, and plays as loud as he can possibly, and she continues crying out.

[Enter the **MUFTI**, in his Night-gown, and two **SERVANTS**.

MUFTI
O thou villain, what horrible impiety art thou committing! what, ravishing the wife of my bosom!—Take him away; ganch him[5], impale him, rid the world of such a monster!

[**SERVANTS** seize him.

ANTONIO
Mercy, dear master, mercy! hear me first, and after, if I have deserved hanging, spare me not. What have you seen to provoke you to this cruelty?

MUFTI
I have heard the outcries of my wife; the bleatings of the poor innocent lamb.—Seen nothing, sayst thou? If I see the lamb lie bleeding, and the butcher by her with his knife drawn, and bloody, is not that evidence sufficient of the murder? I come too late, and the execution is already done.

ANTONIO
Pray think in reason, sir; is a man to be put to death for a similitude? No violence has been committed; none intended; the lamb's alive: and, if I durst tell you so, no more a lamb than I am a butcher.

JOHAYMA
How's that, villain, dar'st thou accuse me?

ANTONIO
Be patient, madam, and speak but truth, and I'll do any thing to serve you: I say again, and swear it too, I'll do any thing to serve you. [Aside.

JOHAYMA [Aside.]
I understand him; but I fear it is now too late to save him:—Pray, hear him speak, husband; perhaps he may say something for himself; I know not.

MUFTI
Speak thou, has he not violated my bed, and thy honour?

JOHAYMA
I forgive him freely, for he has done nothing. What he will do hereafter to make me satisfaction, himself best knows.

ANTONIO
Any thing, any thing, sweet madam: I shall refuse no drudgery.

MUFTI
But did he mean no mischief? was he endeavouring nothing?

JOHAYMA
In my conscience, I begin to doubt he did not.

MUFTI
It's impossible:—then what meant all those outcries?

JOHAYMA
I heard music in the garden, and at an unseasonable time of night; and I stole softly out of my bed, as imagining it might be he.

MUFTI
How's that, Johayma? imagining it was he, and yet you went?

JOHAYMA
Why not, my lord? am not I the mistress of the family? and is it not my place to see good order kept in it? I thought he might have allured some of the she-slaves to him, and was resolved to prevent what might have been betwixt him and them; when, on the sudden, he rushed out upon me, caught me in his arms with such a fury—

MUFTI
I have heard enough.—Away with him!

JOHAYMA
Mistaking me, no doubt, for one of his fellow-slaves: with that, affrighted as I was, I discovered myself, and cried aloud; but as soon as ever he knew me, the villain let me go; and I must needs say, he started back as if I were some serpent; and was more afraid of me than I of him.

MUFTI
O thou corrupter of my family, that's cause enough of death!—once again, away with him.

JOHAYMA
What, for an intended trespass? No harm has been done, whatever may be. He cost you five hundred crowns, I take it.

MUFTI
Thou say'st true, a very considerable sum: he shall not die, though he had committed folly with a slave; it is too much to lose by him.

ANTONIO
My only fault has ever been to love playing in the dark; and the more she cried, the more I played, that it might be seen I intended nothing to her.

MUFTI
To your kennel, sirrah; mortify your flesh, and consider in whose family you are.

JOHAYMA
And one thing more,—remember from henceforth to obey better.

MUFTI [Aside.]
For all her smoothness, I am not quite cured of my jealousy; but I have thought of a way that will clear my doubts.

[Exit **MUFTI** with **JOHAYMA** and **SERVANTS**.

ANTONIO
I am mortified sufficiently already, without the help of his ghostly counsel. Fear of death has gone farther with me in two minutes, than my conscience would have gone in two months. I find myself in a very dejected condition, all over me; poor sin lies dormant; concupiscence is retired to his winter-quarters; and if Morayma should now appear,—I say no more; but, alas for her and me!

[**MORAYMA** comes out of the Arbour, she steals behind him, and claps him on the Back.

MORAYMA
And if Morayma should appear, as she does appear,—alas! You say, for her and you.

ANTONIO
Art thou there, my sweet temptation! my eyes, my life, my soul, my all!

MORAYMA
A mighty compliment! when all these, by your own confession, are just nothing.

ANTONIO
Nothing, till thou camest to new create me; thou dost not know the power of thy own charms: Let me embrace thee, and thou shalt see how quickly I can turn wicked.

MORAYMA [Stepping back.]
Nay, if you are so dangerous, it is best keeping you at a distance, I have no mind to warm a frozen snake in my bosom; he may chance to recover, and sting me for my pains.

ANTONIO
Consider what I have suffered for thy sake already, and make me some amends; two disappointments in a night: O cruel creature!

MORAYMA
And you may thank yourself for both. I came eagerly to the charge before my time, through the back-walk behind the arbour; and you, like a fresh-water soldier, stood guarding the pass before. If you missed the enemy, you may thank your own dulness.

ANTONIO
Nay, if you will be using stratagems, you shall give me leave to make use of my advantages, now I have you in my power: we are fairly met; I'll try it out, and give no quarter.

MORAYMA

By your favour, sir, we meet upon treaty now, and not upon defiance.

ANTONIO
If that be all, you shall have carte blanche immediately; for I long to be ratifying.

MORAYMA
No; now I think on't, you are already entered into articles with my enemy Johayma:—"Any thing to serve you, madam; I shall refuse no drudgery:"—Whose words were those, gentleman? was that like a cavalier of honour?

ANTONIO
Not very heroic; but self-preservation is a point above honour and religion too. Antonio was a rogue, I must confess; but you must give me leave to love him.

MORAYMA
To beg your life so basely, and to present your sword to your enemy; Oh, recreant!

ANTONIO
If I had died honourably, my fame indeed would have sounded loud, but I should never have heard the blast:—Come, don't make yourself worse-natured than you are; to save my life, you would be content I should promise any thing.

MORAYMA
Yes, if I were sure you would perform nothing.

ANTONIO
Can you suspect I would leave you for Johayma?

MORAYMA
No; but I can expect you would have both of us. Love is covetous; I must have all of you; heart for heart is an equal trick. In short, I am younger, I think handsomer, and am sure I love you better. She has been my stepmother these fifteen years: You think that is her face you see, but it is only a daubed vizard; she wears an armour of proof upon it; an inch thick of paint, besides the wash. Her face is so fortified, that you can make no approaches to it without a shovel; but, for her constancy, I can tell you for your comfort, she will love till death, I mean till yours; for when she has worn you out, she will certainly dispatch you to another world, for fear of telling tales, as she has already served three slaves, your predecessors, of happy memory, in her favours. She has made my pious father a three-piled cuckold to my knowledge; and now she would be robbing me of my single sheep too.

ANTONIO
Pr'ythee, prevent her then; and at least take the shearing of me first.

MORAYMA
No; I'll have a butcher's pennyworth of you; first secure the carcase, and then take the fleece into the bargain.

ANTONIO
Why, sure, you did not put yourself and me to all this trouble for a dry come-off; by this hand—

[Taking it.

MORAYMA
Which you shall never touch, but upon better assurances than you imagine.

[Pulling her hand away.

ANTONIO
I'll marry thee, and make a Christian of thee, thou pretty damned infidel.

MORAYMA
I mean you shall; but no earnest till the bargain be made before witness: there is love enough to be had, and as much as you can turn you to, never doubt; but all upon honourable terms.

ANTONIO
I vow and swear by Love; and he's a deity in all religions.

MORAYMA
But never to be trusted in any: he has another name too, of a worse sound. Shall I trust an oath, when I see your eyes languishing, your cheeks flushing, and can hear your heart throbbing? No, I'll not come near you: he's a foolish physician, who will feel the pulse of a patient, that has the plague-spots upon him.

ANTONIO
Did one ever hear a little moppet argue so perversely against so good a cause! Come, pr'ythee, let me anticipate a little of my revenue.

MORAYMA
You would fain be fingering your rents before-hand; but that makes a man an ill husband ever after. Consider, marriage is a painful vocation, as you shall prove it; manage your incomes as thriftily as you can, you shall find a hard task on't to make even at the year's end, and yet to live decently.

ANTONIO
I came with a Christian intention to revenge myself upon thy father, for being the head of a false religion.

MORAYMA
And so you shall; I offer you his daughter for your second. But since you are so pressing, meet me under my window to-morrow night, body for body, about this hour; I'll slip down out of my lodging, and bring my father in my hand.

ANTONIO
How, thy father!

MORAYMA
I mean, all that's good of him; his pearls and jewels, his whole contents, his heart and soul; as much as ever I can carry! I'll leave him his Alcoran, that's revenue enough for him; every page of it is gold and

diamonds. He has the turn of an eye, a demure smile, and a godly cant, that are worth millions to him. I forgot to tell you, that I will have a slave prepared at the postern gate, with two horses ready saddled.—No more, for I fear I may be missed; and think I hear them calling for me.—If you have constancy and courage—

ANTONIO
Never doubt it; and love in abundance, to wander with thee all the world over.

MORAYMA
The value of twelve hundred thousand crowns in a casket!—

ANTONIO
A heavy burden, heaven knows! but we must pray for patience to
support it.

MORAYMA
Besides a willing titt, that will venture her corps with you. Come, I know you long to have a parting blow with me; and therefore, to shew I am in charity—

[He kisses her.

ANTONIO
Once more for pity, that I may keep the flavour upon my lips till we meet again.

MORAYMA
No, frequent charities make bold beggars; and, besides, I have learned of a falconer, never to feed up a hawk when I would have him fly. That's enough; but, if you would be nibbling, here's a hand to stay your stomach.

[Kissing her hand.

ANTONIO
Thus conquered infidels, that wars may cease,
Are forced to give their hands, and sign the peace.

MORAYMA
Thus Christians are outwitted by the foe;
You had her in your power, and let her go.
If you release my hand, the fault's not mine;
You should have made me seal, as well as sign.

[She runs off, he follows her to the door; then comes back again, and goes out at the other.

ACT IV

SCENE I.—Benducar's Palace, in the Castle of Alcazar

BENDUCAR solus.

BENDUCAR
My future fate, the colour of my life,
My all, depends on this important hour:
This hour my lot is weighing in the scales,
And heaven, perhaps, is doubting what to do.
Almeyda and a crown have pushed me forward:
'Tis fixed, the tyrant must not ravish her;
He and Sebastian stand betwixt my hopes;
He most, and therefore first to be dispatched.
These, and a thousand things, are to be done
In the short compass of this rolling night;
And nothing yet performed,
None of my emissaries yet returned.

[Enter **HALY**, first Servant.

Oh Haly, thou hast held me long in pain.
What hast thou learnt of Dorax? is he dead?

HALY
Two hours I warily have watched his palace;
All doors are shut, no servant peeps abroad;
Some officers, with striding haste, passed in,
While others outward went on quick dispatch.
Sometimes hushed silence seemed to reign within;
Then cries confused, and a joint clamour, followed;
Then lights went gliding by, from room to room,
And shot, like thwarting meteors, cross the house.
Not daring further to inquire, I came
With speed, to bring you this imperfect news.

BENDUCAR
Hence I conclude him either dead, or dying.
His mournful friends, summoned to take their leaves,
Are thronged about his couch, and sit in council.
What those caballing captains may design,
I must prevent, by being first in action.—
To Muley-Zeydan fly with speed, desire him
To take my last instructions; tell the importance,
And haste his presence here.—

[Exit **HALY**.

How has this poison lost its wonted way?
It should have burnt its passage, not have lingered

In the blind labyrinths and crooked turnings
Of human composition; now it moves
Like a slow fire, that works against the wind,
As if his stronger stars had interposed.—

[Enter **HAMET**.

Well, Hamet, are our friends, the rabble, raised?
From Mustapha what message?

HAMET
What you wish.
The streets are thicker in this noon of night,
Than at the mid-day sun; a drowsy horror
Sits on their eyes, like fear, not well awake;
All crowd in heaps, as, at a night alarm,
The bees drive out upon each others backs,
To imboss their hives in clusters; all ask news;
Their busy captain runs the weary round,
To whisper orders; and, commanding silence,
Makes not noise cease, but deafens it to murmurs.

BENDUCAR
Night wastes apace; when, when will he appear!

HAMET
He only waits your summons.

BENDUCAR
Haste their coming.
Let secrecy and silence be enjoined
In their close march. What news from the lieutenant?

HAMET
I left him at the gate, firm to your interest,
To admit the townsmen at their first appearance.

BENDUCAR
Thus far 'tis well: Go, hasten Mustapha.

[Exit **HAMET**.

[Enter **ORCHAN**, the third Servant.

O, Orchan, did I think thy diligence
Would lag behind the rest!—What from the Mufti?

ORCHAN

I sought him round his palace; made inquiry
Of all the slaves; in short, I used your name,
And urged the importance home; but had for answer,
That, since the shut of evening, none had seen him.

BENDUCAR
O the curst fate of all conspiracies!
They move on many springs; if one but fail,
The restiff machine stops. In an ill hour he's absent;
'Tis the first time, and sure will be the last,
That e'er a Mufti was not in the way,
When tumults and rebellion should be broached.
Stay by me; thou art resolute and faithful;
I have employment worthy of thy arm.

[Walks.

[Enter **MULEY-ZEYDAN**.

MULEY-ZEYDAN
You see me come, impatient of my hopes,
And eager as the courser for the race:
Is all in readiness?

BENDUCAR
All but the Mufti.

MULEY-ZEYDAN
We must go on without him.

BENDUCAR
True, we must;
For 'tis ill stopping in the full career,
Howe'er the leap be dangerous and wide.

ORCHAN [Looking out.]
I see the blaze of torches from afar,
And hear the trampling of thick-beating feet;
This way they move.

BENDUCAR
No doubt, the emperor.
We must not be surprised in conference.
Trust to my management the tyrant's death,
And haste yourself to join with Mustapha.
The officer, who guards the gate, is yours:
When you have gained that pass, divide your force;
Yourself in person head one chosen half,

And march to oppress the faction in consult
With dying Dorax. Fate has driven them all
Into the net; you must be bold and sudden:
Spare none; and if you find him struggling yet
With pangs of death, trust not his rolling eyes
And heaving gasps; for poison may be false,—
The home thrust of a friendly sword is sure.

MULEY-ZEYDAN
Doubt not my conduct; they shall be surprised.
Mercy may wait without the gate one night,
At morn I'll take her in.

BENDUCAR
Here lies your way;
You meet your brother there.

MULEY-ZEYDAN
May we ne'er meet!
For, like the twins of Leda, when I mount,
He gallops down the skies.

[Exit **MULEY- ZEYDAN**.

BENDUCAR
He comes:—Now, heart,
Be ribbed with iron for this one attempt;
Set ope thy sluices, send the vigorous blood
Through every active limb for my relief;
Then take thy rest within thy quiet cell,
For thou shalt drum no more.

[Enter **EMPEROR**, and **GUARDS** attending him.

EMPEROR
What news of our affairs, and what of Dorax?
Is he no more? say that, and make me happy.

BENDUCAR
May all your enemies be like that dog,
Whose parting soul is labouring at the lips.

EMPEROR
The people, are they raised?

BENDUCAR
And marshalled too;
Just ready for the march.

EMPEROR
Then I'm at ease.

BENDUCAR
The night is yours; the glittering host of heaven
Shines but for you; but most the star of love,
That twinkles you to fair Almeyda's bed.
Oh, there's a joy to melt in her embrace,
Dissolve in pleasure,
And make the gods curse immortality,
That so they could not die.
But haste, and make them yours.

EMPEROR
I will; and yet
A kind of weight hangs heavy at my heart;
My flagging soul flies under her own pitch,
Like fowl in air too damp, and lugs along,
As if she were a body in a body,
And not a mounting substance made of fire.
My senses, too, are dull and stupified,
Their edge rebated:—sure some ill approaches,
And some kind sprite knocks softly at my soul,
To tell me, fate's at hand[6].

BENDUCAR
Mere fancies all.
Your soul has been before-hand with your body,
And drunk so deep a draught of promised bliss,
She slumbers o'er the cup; no danger's near,
But of a surfeit at too full a feast.

EMPEROR
It may be so; it looks so like the dream
That overtook me, at my waking hour,
This morn; and dreams, they say, are then divine,
When all the balmy vapours are exhaled,
And some o'erpowering god continues sleep.
'Twas then, methought, Almeyda, smiling, came,
Attended with a train of all her race,
Whom, in the rage of empire, I had murdered:
But now, no longer foes, they gave me joy
Of my new conquest, and, with helping hands,
Heaved me into our holy prophet's arms,
Who bore me in a purple cloud to heaven[7].

BENDUCAR

Good omen, sir; I wish you in that heaven
Your dream portends you,—
Which presages death. [Aside.

EMPEROR
Thou too wert there;
And thou, methought, didst push me from below,
With thy full force, to Paradise.

BENDUCAR
Yet better.

EMPEROR
Ha! what's that grizly fellow, that attends thee?

BENDUCAR
Why ask you, sir?

EMPEROR
For he was in my dream,
And helped to heave me up.

BENDUCAR
With prayers and wishes;
For I dare swear him honest.

EMPEROR
That may be;
But yet he looks damnation.

BENDUCAR
You forget
The face would please you better. Do you love,
And can you thus forbear?

EMPEROR
I'll head my people,
Then think of dalliance when the danger's o'er.
My warlike spirits work now another way,
And my soul's tuned to trumpets.

BENDUCAR
You debase yourself,
To think of mixing with the ignoble herd;
Let such perform the servile work of war,
Such who have no Almeyda to enjoy.
What, shall the people know their god-like prince
Skulked in a nightly skirmish? Stole a conquest,

Headed a rabble, and profaned his person,
Shouldered with filth, borne in a tide of ordure,
And stifled with their rank offensive sweat?

EMPEROR
I am off again; I will not prostitute
The regal dignity so far, to head them.

BENDUCAR
There spoke a king.
Dismiss your guards, to be employed elsewhere
In ruder combats; you will want no seconds
In those alarms you seek.

EMPEROR
Go, join the crowd;—[To the **GUARDS**.
Benducar, thou shalt lead them in my place.

[Exeunt **GUARDS**.

The God of Love once more has shot his fires
Into my soul, and my whole heart receives him.
Almeyda now returns with all her charms;
I feel her as she glides along my veins,
And dances in my blood. So when our prophet
Had long been hammering, in his lonely cell,
Some dull, insipid, tedious Paradise,
A brisk Arabian girl came tripping by;
Passing she cast at him a side-long glance,
And looked behind, in hopes to be pursued:
He took the hint, embraced the flying fair,
And, having found his heaven, he fixed it there.

[Exit **EMPEROR**.

BENDUCAR
That Paradise thou never shalt possess.
His death is easy now, his guards are gone,
And I can sin but once to seize the throne;
All after-acts are sanctified by power.

ORCHAN
Command my sword and life.

BENDUCAR
I thank thee, Orchan,
And shall reward thy faith. This master-key
Frees every lock, and leads us to his person;

And, should we miss our blow,—as heaven forbid!—
Secures retreat. Leave open all behind us;
And first set wide the Mufti's garden gate,
Which is his private passage to the palace;
For there our mutineers appoint to meet,
And thence we may have aid.—Now sleep, ye stars,
That silently o'erwatch the fate of kings!
Be all propitious influences barred,
And none but murderous planets mount the guard.

[Exit with **ORCHAN**.

SCENE II.—A Night-Scene of the Mufti's Garden

Enter the **MUFTI** alone, in a Slave's Habit, like that of **ANTONIO**.

MUFTI
This it is to have a sound head-piece; by this I have got to be chief of my religion; that is, honestly speaking, to teach others what I neither know nor believe myself. For what's Mahomet to me, but that I get by him? Now for my policy of this night: I have mewed up my suspected spouse in her chamber;—no more embassies to that lusty young stallion of a gardener. Next, my habit of a slave; I have made myself as like him as I can, all but his youth and vigour; which when I had, I passed my time as well as any of my holy predecessors. Now, walking under the windows of my seraglio, if Johayma look out, she will certainly take me for Antonio, and call to me; and by that I shall know what concupiscence is working in her. She cannot come down to commit iniquity, there's my safety; but if she peep, if she put her nose abroad, there's demonstration of her pious will; and I'll not make the first precedent for a churchman to forgive injuries.

[Enter **MORAYMA**, running to him with a Casket in her hand, and embracing him.

MORAYMA
Now I can embrace you with a good conscience; here are the pearls and jewels, here's my father.

MUFTI
I am indeed thy father; but how the devil didst thou know me in this disguise? and what pearls and jewels dost thou mean?

MORAYMA [Going back.]
What have I done, and what will now become of me!

MUFTI
Art thou mad, Morayma?

MORAYMA
I think you'll make me so.

MUFTI

Why, what have I done to thee? Recollect thyself, and speak sense to me.

MORAYMA
Then give me leave to tell you, you are the worst of fathers.

MUFTI
Did I think I had begotten such a monster!—Proceed, my dutiful child, proceed, proceed.

MORAYMA
You have been raking together a mass of wealth, by indirect and wicked means: the spoils of orphans are in these jewels, and the tears of widows in these pearls.

MUFTI
Thou amazest me!

MORAYMA
I would do so. This casket is loaded with your sins; 'tis the cargo of rapines, simony, and extortions; the iniquity of thirty years muftiship converted into diamonds.

MUFTI
Would some rich railing rogue would say as much to me, that I might squeeze his purse for scandal!

MORAYMA
No, sir, you get more by pious fools than railers, when you insinuate into their families, manage their fortunes while they live, and beggar their heirs, by getting legacies, when they die. And do you think I'll be the receiver of your theft? I discharge my conscience of it: Here, take again your filthy mammon, and restore it, you had best, to the true owners.

MUFTI
I am finely documented by my own daughter!

MORAYMA
And a great credit for me to be so: Do but think how decent a habit you have on, and how becoming your function to be disguised like a slave, and eaves-dropping under the women's windows, to be saluted, as you deserve it richly, with a piss-pot. If I had not known you casually by your shambling gait, and a certain reverend awkwardness that is natural to all of your function, here you had been exposed to the laughter of your own servants; who have been in search of you through the whole seraglio, peeping under every petticoat to find you.

MUFTI
Pr'ythee, child, reproach me no more of human failings; they are but a little of the pitch and spots of the world, that are still sticking on me; but I hope to scour them out in time. I am better at bottom than thou thinkest; I am not the man thou takest me for.

MORAYMA
No, to my sorrow, sir, you are not.

MUFTI

It was a very odd beginning though, methought, to see thee come running in upon me with such a warm embrace; pr'ythee, what was the meaning of that violent hot hug?

MORAYMA
I am sure I meant nothing by it, but the zeal and affection which I bear to the man of the world, whom I may love lawfully.

MUFTI
But thou wilt not teach me, at this age, the nature of a close embrace?

MORAYMA
No, indeed; for my mother-in-law complains, that you are past teaching: But if you mistook my innocent embrace for sin, I wish heartily it had been given where it would have been more acceptable.

MUFTI
Why this is as it should be now; take the treasure again, it can never be put into better hands.

MORAYMA
Yes, to my knowledge, but it might. I have confessed my soul to you, if you can understand me rightly. I never disobeyed you till this night; and now, since, through the violence of my passion, I have been so unfortunate, I humbly beg your pardon, your blessing, and your leave, that, upon the first opportunity, I may go for ever from your sight; for heaven knows, I never desire to see you more.

MUFTI [Wiping his eyes.]
Thou makest me weep at thy unkindness; indeed, dear daughter, we will not part.

MORAYMA
Indeed, dear daddy, but we will.

MUFTI
Why, if I have been a little pilfering, or so, I take it bitterly of thee to tell me of it, since it was to make thee rich; and I hope a man may make bold with his own soul, without offence to his own child. Here, take the jewels again; take them, I charge thee, upon thy obedience.

MORAYMA
Well then, in virtue of obedience, I will take them; but, on my soul, I had rather they were in a better hand.

MUFTI
Meaning mine, I know it.

MORAYMA
Meaning his, whom I love better than my life.

MUFTI
That's me again.

MORAYMA

I would have you think so.

MUFTI
How thy good nature works upon me! Well, I can do no less than venture damning for thee; and I may put fair for it, if the rabble be ordered to rise to-night.

[Enter **ANTONIO**, in a rich African habit.

ANTONIO
What do you mean, my dear, to stand talking in this suspicious place, just underneath Johayma's window?—[To the **MUFTI**] You are well met, comrade; I know you are the friend of our flight: are the horses ready at the postern gate?

MUFTI
Antonio, and in disguise! now I begin to smell a rat.

ANTONIO
And I another, that out-stinks it. False Morayma, hast thou thus betrayed me to thy father!

MORAYMA
Alas! I was betrayed myself. He came disguised like you, and I, poor innocent, ran into his hands.

MUFTI
In good time you did so; I laid a trap for a bitch-fox, and a worse vermin has caught himself in it. You would fain break loose now, though you left a limb behind you; but I am yet in my own territories, and in call of company; that's my comfort.

ANTONIO [Taking him by the throat.]
No; I have a trick left to put thee past thy squeaking. I have given thee the quinsy; that ungracious tongue shall preach no more false doctrine.

MORAYMA
What do you mean? you will not throttle him? consider he's my father.

ANTONIO
Pr'ythee, let us provide first for our own safety; if I do not consider him, he will consider us, with a vengeance, afterwards.

MORAYMA
You may threaten him for crying out; but, for my sake, give him back a little cranny of his windpipe, and some part of speech.

ANTONIO
Not so much as one single interjection.—Come away, father-in-law, this is no place for dialogues; when you are in the mosque, you talk by hours, and there no man must interrupt you. This is but like for like, good father-in-law; now I am in the pulpit, it is your turn to hold your tongue.

[He struggles.]

Nay, if you will be hanging back, I shall take care you shall hang forward.

[Pulls him along the Stage, with his Sword at his Reins.

MORAYMA
The other way to the arbour with him; and make haste, before we are discovered.

ANTONIO
If I only bind and gag him there, he may commend me hereafter for civil usage; he deserves not so much favour by any action of his life.

MORAYMA
Yes, pray bate him one,—for begetting your mistress.

ANTONIO
I would, if he had not thought more of thy mother than of thee. Once more, come along in silence, my Pythagorean father-in-law.

JOHAYMA [At the Balcony.]
A bird in a cage may peep, at least, though she must not fly.—What bustle's there beneath my window? Antonio, by all my hopes! I know him by his habit. But what makes that woman with him, and a friend, a sword drawn, and hasting hence? This is no time for silence:—Who's within? call there, where are the servants? why, Omar, Abedin, Hassan, and the rest, make haste, and run into the garden; there are thieves and villains; arm all the family, and stop them.

ANTONIO [Turning back.]
O that screech owl at the window! we shall be pursued immediately; which way shall we take?

MORAYMA [Giving him the Casket.]
'Tis impossible to escape them; for the way to our horses lies back again by the house, and then we shall meet them full in the teeth. Here, take these jewels; thou mayst leap the walls, and get away.

ANTONIO
And what will become of thee, then, poor kind soul?

MORAYMA
I must take my fortune. When you are got safe into your own country, I hope you will bestow a sigh on the memory of her who loved you.

ANTONIO
It makes me mad to think, how many a good night will be lost betwixt us! Take back thy jewels; 'tis an empty casket without thee: besides, I should never leap well with the weight of all thy father's sins about me; thou and they had been a bargain.

MORAYMA
Pr'ythee take them, 'twill help me to be revenged on him.

ANTONIO
No, they'll serve to make thy peace with him.

MORAYMA
I hear them coming; shift for yourself at least; remember I am yours for ever.

[**SERVANTS** crying, "this way, this way," behind the Scenes.

ANTONIO
And I but the empty shadow of myself without thee!—Farewell, father-in-law, that should have been, if I had not been curst in my mother's belly.—Now, which way, Fortune?

[Runs amazedly backwards and forwards.

SERVANTS within, "Follow, follow; yonder are the villains."
O, here's a gate open; but it leads into the castle; yet I must venture it.

[A shout behind the Scenes, where **ANTONIO** is going out.
There's the rabble in a mutiny; what, is the devil up at midnight!
However, 'tis good herding in a crowd.

[Runs out. **MUFTI** runs to **MORAYMA**, and lays hold on her, then snatches away the Casket.

MUFTI
Now, to do things in order, first I seize upon the bag, and then upon the baggage; for thou art but my flesh and blood, but these are my life and soul.

MORAYMA
Then let me follow my flesh and blood, and keep to yourself your life and soul.

MUFTI
Both, or none; come away to durance.

MORAYMA
Well, if it must be so, agreed; for I have another trick to play you, and thank yourself for what shall follow.

[Enter **SERVANTS**.

JOHAYMA [From above.]
One of them took through the private way into the castle; follow him, be sure, for these are yours already.

MORAYMA
Help here quickly, Omar, Abedin! I have hold on the villain that stole my jewels; but 'tis a lusty rogue, and he will prove too strong for me. What! help, I say; do you not know your master's daughter?

MUFTI

Now, if I cry out, they will know my voice, and then I am disgraced for ever. O thou art a venomous cockatrice!

MORAYMA
Of your own begetting.

[The **SERVANTS** seize him.

1ˢᵀ SERVANT
What a glorious deliverance have you had, madam, from this
bloody-minded Christian!

MORAYMA
Give me back my jewels, and carry this notorious malefactor to be punished by my father.—I'll hunt the other dry-foot.

[Takes the jewels, and runs out after **ANTONIO** at the same passage.

1ˢᵀ SERVANT
I long to be hanselling his hide, before we bring him to my
master.

2ᴺᴰ SERVANT
Hang him, for an old covetous hypocrite; he deserves a worse punishment himself, for keeping us so hardly.

1ˢᵀ SERVANT
Ay, would he were in this villain's place! thus I would lay him on, and thus.

[Beats him.

2ᴺᴰ SERVANT
And thus would I revenge myself of my last beating.

[He beats him too, and then the rest.

MUFTI
Oh, ho, ho!

1ˢᵀ SERVANT
Now, supposing you were the Mufti, sir.—

[Beats him again.

MUFTI
The devil's in that supposing rascal!—I can bear no more; and I am the Mufti. Now suppose yourselves my servants, and hold your hands: an anointed halter take you all!

1ST SERVANT
My master!—You will pardon the excess of our zeal for you, sir: Indeed we all took you for a villain, and so we used you.

MUFTI
Ay, so I feel you did; my back and sides are abundant
testimonies of your zeal.—Run, rogues, and bring me back my jewels,
and my fugitive daughter; run, I say.

[They run to the gate, and the **FIRST SERVANT** runs back again.

1ST SERVANT
Sir, the castle is in a most terrible combustion; you may hear them hither.

MUFTI
'Tis a laudable commotion; the voice of the mobile is the voice of heaven.—I must retire a little, to strip me of the slave, and to assume the Mufti, and then I will return; for the piety of the people must be encouraged, that they may help me to recover my jewels, and my daughter.

[Exeunt **MUFTI** and **SERVANTS**.

SCENE III—Changes to the Castle Yard

And discovers **ANTONIO, MUSTAPHA,** and the **RABBLE** shouting. They come forward.

ANTONIO
And so at length, as I informed you, I escaped out of his covetous clutches; and now fly to your illustrious feet for my protection.

MUSTAPHA
Thou shalt have it, and now defy the Mufti. 'Tis the first petition that has been made to me since my exaltation to tumult, in this second night of the month Abib, and in the year of the Hegira,—the Lord knows what year; but 'tis no matter; for when I am settled, the learned are bound to find it out for me; for I am resolved to date my authority over the rabble, like other monarchs.

ANTONIO
I have always had a longing to be yours again, though I could not compass it before; and had designed you a casket of my master's jewels too; for I knew the custom, and would not have appeared before a great person, as you are, without a present: But he has defrauded my good intentions, and basely robbed you of them; 'tis a prize worthy a million of crowns, and you carry your letters of marque about you.

MUSTAPHA
I shall make bold with his treasure, for the support of my new government.—

[The **PEOPLE** gather about him.]

—What do these vile raggamuffins so near our person? your savour is offensive to us; bear back there, and make room for honest men to approach us: These fools and knaves are always impudently crowding next to princes, and keeping off the more deserving: Bear back, I say.—

[They make a wider circle.]

—That's dutifully done! Now shout, to shew your loyalty.

[A great shout.]

—Hear'st thou that, slave Antonio? These obstreperous villains shout, and know not for what they make a noise. You shall see me manage them, that you may judge what ignorant beasts they are.—For whom do you shout now? Who's to live and reign; tell me that, the wisest of you?

1ST RABBLE
Even who you please, captain.

MUSTAPHA
La, you there! I told you so.

2ND RABBLE
We are not bound to know, who is to live and reign; our business is only to rise upon command, and plunder.

3RD RABBLE
Ay, the richest of both parties; for they are our enemies.

MUSTAPHA
This last fellow is a little more sensible than the rest; he has entered somewhat into the merits of the cause.

1ST RABBLE
If a poor man may speak his mind. I think, captain, that yourself are the fittest to live and reign; I mean not over, but next, and immediately under, the people; and thereupon I say, A Mustapha, a Muatapha!

OMNES
A Mustapha, a Mustapha!

MUSTAPHA
I must confess the sound is pleasing, and tickles the ears of my ambition; but alas, good people, it must not be! I am contented to be a poor simple viceroy. But prince Muley-Zeydan is to be the man: I shall take care to instruct him in the arts of government, and in his duty to us all; and, therefore, mark my cry, A Muley-Zeydan, a Muley-Zeydan!

OMNES
A Muley-Zeydan, a Muley-Zeydan!

MUSTAPHA

You see, slave Antonio, what I might have been?

ANTONIO
I observe your modesty.

MUSTAPHA
But for a foolish promise, I made once to my lord Benducar, to set up any one he pleased.—

[Re-enter the **MUFTI**, with his **SERVANTS**.

ANTONIO
Here's the old hypocrite again.—Now stand your ground and bate him not an inch. Remember the jewels, the rich and glorious jewels; they are designed to be yours, by virtue of prerogative.

MUSTAPHA
Let me alone to pick a quarrel; I have an old grudge to him
upon thy account.

MUFTI [Making up to the Mobile.]
Good people, here you are met together.

1ST RABLE
Ay, we know that without your telling: But why are we met together, doctor? for that's it which no body here can tell.

2ND RABBLE
Why, to see one another in the dark; and to make holiday at midnight.

MUFTI
You are met, as becomes good Mussulmen, to settle the nation; for I must tell you, that, though your tyrant is a lawful emperor, yet your lawful emperor is but a tyrant.

ANTONIO
What stuff he talks!

MUSTAPHA
'Tis excellent fine matter, indeed, slave Antonio! He has a rare tongue! Oh, he would move a rock, or elephant!

ANTONIO
What a block have I to work upon! [Aside.]—But still, remember the jewels, sir; the jewels.

MUSTAPHA
Nay, that's true, on the other side; the jewels must be mine. But he has a pure fine way of talking; my conscience goes along with him, but the jewels have set my heart against him.

MUFTI

That your emperor is a tyrant, is most manifest; for you were born to be Turks, but he has played the Turk with you, and is taking your religion away.

2ND RABBLE
We find that in our decay of trade. I have seen, for these hundred years, that religion and trade always go together.

MUFTI
He is now upon the point of marrying himself, without your sovereign consent: And what are the effects of marriage?

3RD RABBLE
A scolding domineering wife, if she prove honest; and, if a whore, a fine gaudy minx, that robs our counters every night, and then goes out, and spends it upon our cuckold-makers.

MUFTI
No; the natural effects of marriage are children: Now, on whom would he beget these children? Even upon a Christian! O, horrible! how can you believe me, though I am ready to swear it upon the Alcoran! Yes, true believers, you may believe, that he is going to beget a race of misbelievers.

MUSTAPHA
That's fine, in earnest; I cannot forbear hearkening to his enchanting tongue.

ANTONIO
But yet remember—

MUSTAPHA
Ay, ay, the jewels! Now again I hate him; but yet my conscience makes me listen to him.

MUFTI
Therefore, to conclude all, believers, pluck up your hearts, and pluck down the tyrant. Remember the courage of your ancestors; remember the majesty of the people; remember yourselves, your wives, and children; and, lastly, above all, remember your religion, and our holy Mahomet. All these require your timeous assistance;—shall I say, they beg it? No; they claim it of you, by all the nearest and dearest ties of these three P's, self-preservation, our property, and our prophet.—Now answer me with an unanimous cheerful cry, and follow me, who am your leader, to a glorious deliverance.

OMNES
A Mufti, a Mufti!

[Following him off the stage.

ANTONIO
Now you see what comes of your foolish qualms of conscience; the jewels are lost, and they are all leaving you.

MUSTAPHA

What, am I forsaken of my subjects? Would the rogue purloin my liege people from me!—I charge you, in my own name, come back, ye deserters, and hear me speak.

1ST RABBLE
What, will he come with his balderdash, after the Mufti's eloquent oration?

2ND RABBLE
He's our captain, lawfully picked up, and elected upon a stall; we will hear him.

OMNES
Speak, captain, for we will hear you.

MUSTAPHA
Do you remember the glorious rapines and robberies you have committed? Your breaking open and gutting of houses, your rummaging of cellars, your demolishing of Christian temples, and bearing off, in triumph, the superstitious plate and pictures, the ornaments of their wicked altars, when all rich moveables were sentenced for idolatrous, and all that was idolatrous was seized? Answer first, for your remembrance of all these sweetnesses of mutiny; for upon those grounds I shall proceed.

OMNES
Yes, we do remember, we do remember.

MUSTAPHA
Then make much of your retentive faculties.—And who led you to those honey-combs? Your Mufti? No, believers; he only preached you up to it, but durst not lead you: He was but your counsellor, but I was your captain; he only looed you, but, 'twas I that led you.

OMNES
That's true, that's true.

ANTONIO
There you were with him for his figures.

MUSTAPHA
I think I was, slave Antonio. Alas, I was ignorant of my own talent!—Say then, believers, will you have a captain for your Mufti, or a Mufti for your captain? And, further, to instruct you how to cry, will you have A mufti, or No mufti?

OMNES
No Mufti, no Mufti!

MUSTAPHA
That I laid in for them, slave Antonio—Do I then spit upon your faces? Do I discourage rebellion, mutiny, rapine, and plundering? You may think I do, believers; but, heaven forbid! No, I encourage you to all these laudable undertakings; you shall plunder, you shall pull down the government; but you shall do this upon my authority, and not by his wicked instigation.

3RD RABBLE

Nay, when his turn is served, he may preach up loyalty again, and restitution, that he might have another snack among us.

1ˢᵀ RABBLE
He may indeed; for it is but his saying it is sin, and then we must restore; and therefore I would have a new religion, where half the commandments should be taken away, the rest mollified, and there should be little or no sin remaining.

OMNES
Another religion, a new religion, another religion!

MUSTAPHA
And that may easily be done, with the help of a little inspiration; for I must tell you, I have a pigeon at home, of Mahomet's own breed; and when I have learnt her to pick pease out of my ear, rest satisfied till then, and you shall have another. But, now I think on't, I am inspired already, that 'tis no sin to depose the Mufti.

ANTONIO
And good reason; for when kings and queens are to be discarded, what should knaves do any longer in the pack?

OMNES
He is deposed, he is deposed, he is deposed!

MUSTAPHA
Nay, if he and his clergy will needs be preaching up rebellion, and giving us their blessing, 'tis but justice they should have the first-fruits of it.—Slave Antonio, take him into custody; and dost thou hear, boy, be sure to secure the little transitory box of jewels. If he be obstinate, put a civil question to him upon the rack, and he squeaks, I warrant him.

ANTONIO [Seizing the **MUFTI**]
Come, my quondam master, you and I must change qualities.

MUFTI
I hope you will not be so barbarous to torture me: we may preach suffering to others, but, alas! holy flesh is too well pampered to endure martyrdom.

MUSTAPHA
Now, late Mufti, not forgetting my first quarrel to you, we will enter ourselves with the plunder of your palace: 'tis good to sanctify a work, and begin a God's name.

1ˢᵀ RABBLE
Our prophet let the devil alone with the last mob.

MOB
But he takes care of this himself.

As they are going out, enter **BENDUCAR**, *leading* **ALMEYDA**: *he with a sword in one hand;* **BENDUCAR'S** *Slave follows, with* **MULEY-MOLUCH'S** *head upon a spear.*

MUSTAPHA
Not so much haste, masters; comeback again; you are so bent upon mischief, that you take a man upon the first word of plunder. Here is a sight for you; the emperor is come upon his head to visit you.

[Bowing.]

Most noble emperor, now I hope you will not hit us in the teeth, that we have pulled you down; for we can tell you to your face, that we have exalted you.

[They all shout.

BENDUCAR
Think what I am, and what yourself may be,
[To **ALMEYDA** apart.
In being mine: refuse not proffered love,
That brings a crown.

ALMEYDA [To him.]
I have resolved,
And these shall know my thoughts.

BENDUCAR [To her.]
On that I build.—

[He comes up to the **RABBLE**.

Joy to the people for the tyrant's death!
Oppression, rapine, banishment, and blood,
Are now no more; but speechless as that tongue,
That lies for ever still.
How is my grief divided with my joy,
When I must own I killed him! Bid me speak;
For not to bid me, is to disallow
What for your sakes is done.

MUSTAPHA
In the name of the people, we command you speak: but that pretty lady shall speak first; for we have taken somewhat of a liking to her person.—Be not afraid, lady, to speak to these rude raggamuffians; there is nothing shall offend you, unless it be their stink, an't please you.

[Making a leg.

ALMEYDA
Why should I fear to speak, who am your queen?
My peaceful father swayed the sceptre long,

And you enjoyed the blessings of his reign,
While you deserved the name of Africans.
Then, not commanded, but commanding you,
Fearless I speak: know me for what I am.

BENDUCAR
How she assumes! I like not this beginning. [Aside.

ALMEYDA
I was not born so base to flatter crowds,
And move your pity by a whining tale.
Your tyrant would have forced me to his bed;
But in the attempt of that foul brutal act,
These loyal slaves secured me by his death.

[Pointing to **BENDUCAR**.

BENDUCAR
Makes she no more of me than of a slave?— [Aside.
Madam, I thought I had instructed you [To **ALMEYDA**.
To frame a speech more suiting to the times:
The circumstances of that dire design,
Your own despair, my unexpected aid,
My life endangered by his bold defence,
And, after all, his death, and your deliverance,
Were themes that ought not to be slighted o'er.

MUSTAPHA
She might have passed over all your petty businesses, and no great matter; but the raising of my rabble is an exploit of consequence, and not to be mumbled up in silence, for all her pertness.

ALMEYDA
When force invades the gift of nature, life,
The eldest law of nature bids defend;
And if in that defence a tyrant fall,
His death's his crime, not ours,
Suffice it, that he's dead; all wrongs die with him;
When he can wrong no more, I pardon him:
Thus I absolve myself, and him excuse,
Who saved my life and honour, but praise neither.

BENDUCAR
'Tis cheap to pardon, whom you would not pay.
But what speak I of payment and reward!
Ungrateful woman, you are yet no queen,
Nor more than a proud haughty christian slave:
As such I seize my right.

[Going to lay hold of her.

ALMEYDA [Drawing a Dagger.]
Dare not to approach me!—
Now, Africans,
He shows himself to you; to me he stood
Confessed before, and owned his insolence
To espouse my person, and assume the crown,
Claimed in my right; for this, he slew your tyrant;
Oh no! he only changed him for a worse;
Embased your slavery by his own vileness,
And loaded you with more ignoble bonds.
Then think me not ungrateful, not to share
The imperial crown with a presuming traitor.
He says, I am a Christian; true, I am,
But yet no slave: If Christians can be thought
Unfit to govern those of other faith,
'Tis left for you to judge.

BENDUCAR
I have not patience; she consumes the time
In idle talk, and owns her false belief:
Seize her by force, and bear her thence unheard.

ALMEYDA [To the **PEOPLE**]
No, let me rather die your sacrifice,
Than live his triumph.
I throw myself into my people's arms;
As you are men, compassionate my wrongs,
And, as good men, protect me.

ANTONIO
Something must be done to save her. [Aside to **MUSTAPHA**] This is all addressed to you, sir: she singled you out with her eye, as commander in chief of the mobility.

MUSTAPHA
Think'st thou so, slave Antonio?

ANTONIO
Most certainly, sir; and you cannot, in honour, but protect her: now look to your hits, and make your fortune.

MUSTAPHA
Methought, indeed, she cast a kind leer towards me. Our prophet was but just such another scoundrel as I am, till he raised himself to power, and consequently to holiness, by marrying his master's widow. I am resolved I'll put forward for myself; for why should I be my lord Benducar's fool and slave, when I may be my own fool and his master?

BENDUCAR
Take her into possession, Mustapha.

MUSTAPHA
That's better counsel than you meant it: Yes, I do take her into possession, and into protection too. What say you, masters, will you stand by me?

OMNES
One and all, one and all.

BENDUCAR
Hast thou betrayed me, traitor?—Mufti, speak, and mind them of religion.

[**MUFTI** shakes his head.

MUSTAPHA
Alas! the poor gentleman has gotten a cold with a sermon of two hours long, and a prayer of fear; and, besides, if he durst speak, mankind is grown wiser at this time of day than to cut one another's throats about religion. Our Mufti's is a green coat, and the Christian's is a black coat; and we must wisely go together by the ears, whether green or black shall sweep our spoils.

[Drums within, and shouts.

BENDUCAR
Now we shall see whose numbers will prevail:
The conquering troops of Muley-Zeydan come,
To crush rebellion, and espouse my cause.

MUSTAPHA
We will have a fair trial of skill for it, I can tell him
that. When we have dispatched with Muley-Zeydan, your lordship shall
march, in equal proportions of your body, to the four gates of the
city, and every tower shall have a quarter of you.

[**ANTONIO** draws them up, and takes **ALMEYDA** by the hand. Shouts again, and Drums.

[Enter **DORAX** and **SEBASTIAN**, attended by African **SOLDIERS** and **PORTUGUESES**. **ALMEYDA** and **SEBASTIAN** run into each others arms, and both speak together.

SEBASTIAN and **ALMEYDA**
My Sebastian! my Almeyda!

ALMEYDA
Do you then live?

SEBASTIAN
And live to love thee ever.

BENDUCAR
How! Dorax and Sebastian still alive!
The Moors and Christians joined!—I thank thee, prophet.

DORAX
The citadel is ours; and Muley-Zeydan
Safe under guard, but as becomes a prince.
Lay down your arms; such base plebeian blood
Would only stain the brightness of my sword,
And blunt it for some nobler work behind.

MUSTAPHA
I suppose you may put it up without offence to any man here present. For my part, I have been loyal to my sovereign lady, though that villain Benducar, and that hypocrite the Mufti, would have corrupted me; but if those two escape public justice, then I and all my late honest subjects here deserve hanging.

BENDUCAR [To **DORAX**]
I'm sure I did my part to poison thee,
What saint soe'er has soldered thee again:
A dose less hot had burst through ribs of iron.

MUFTI
Not knowing that, I poisoned him once more,
And drenched him with a draught so deadly cold,
That, hadst not thou prevented, had congealed
The channel of his blood, and froze him dry.

BENDUCAR
Thou interposing fool, to mangle mischief,
And think to mend the perfect work of hell!

DORAX
Thus, when heaven pleases, double poisons cure[8].
I will not tax thee of ingratitude
To me, thy friend, who hast betrayed thy prince:
Death he deserved indeed, but not from thee.
But fate, it seems, reserved the worst of men
To end the worst of tyrants.—
Go, bear him to his fate,
And send him to attend his master's ghost.
Let some secure my other poisoning friend,
Whose double diligence preserved my life.

ANTONIO
You are fallen into good hands, father-in-law; your sparkling jewels, and Morayma's eyes, may prove a better bail than you deserve.

MUFTI

The best that can come of me, in this condition, is, to have my life begged first, and then to be begged for a fool afterwards[9].

[Exeunt **ANTONIO**, with the **MUFTI**; and, at the same time, **BENDUCAR** is carried off.

DORAX [To **MUSTAPHA**]
You, and your hungry herd, depart untouched;
For justice cannot stoop so low, to reach
The groveling sin of crowds: but curst be they,
Who trust revenge with such mad instruments,
Whose blindfold business is but to destroy;
And, like the fire, commissioned by the winds,
Begins on sheds, but, rolling in a round,
On palaces returns. Away, ye scum,
That still rise upmost when the nation boils;
Ye mongrel work of heaven, with human shapes,
Not to be damned or saved, but breathe and perish,
That have but just enough of sense, to know
The master's voice, when rated, to depart.

[Exeunt **MUSTAPHA** and **RABBLE**.

ALMEYDA
With gratitude as low as knees can pay

[Kneeling to him.

To those blest holy fires, our guardian angels,
Receive these thanks, till altars can be raised.

DORAX
Arise, fair excellence, and pay no thanks,

[Raising her up.

Till time discover what I have deserved.

SEBASTIAN
More than reward can answer.
If Portugal and Spain were joined to Africa,
And the main ocean crusted into land,
If universal monarchy were mine,
Here should the gift be placed.

DORAX
And from some hands I should refuse that gift.
Be not too prodigal of promises;
But stint your bounty to one only grant,

Which I can ask with honour.

SEBASTIAN
What I am
Is but thy gift; make what thou canst of me,
Secure of no repulse.

DORAX
[To **SEBASTIAN**] Dismiss your train.—
[To **ALMEYDA**] You, madam, please one moment to retire.

[**SEBASTIAN** signs to the **PORTUGUESES** to go off; **ALMEYDA**, bowing to him, gives off also. The **AFRICANS** follow her.

DORAX [To the **CAPTAIN** of the Guard.]
With you one word in private.

[Goes out with the **CAPTAIN**.

SEBASTIAN [Solus.]
Reserved behaviour, open nobleness,
A long mysterious track of stern bounty:
But now the hand of fate is on the curtain,
And draws the scene to sight.

[Re-enter **DORAX**, having taken off his Turban, and put on a Peruke, Hat, and Cravat.

DORAX
Now, do you know me?

SEBASTIAN
Thou shouldst be Alonzo.

DORAX
So you should be Sebastian:
But when Sebastian ceased to be himself,
I ceased to be Alonzo.

SEBASTIAN
As in a dream,
I see thee here, and scarce believe mine eyes.

DORAX
Is it so strange to find me, where my wrongs,
And your inhuman tyranny, have sent me?
Think not you dream; or, if you did, my injuries
Shall call so loud, that lethargy should wake,
And death should give you back to answer me.

A thousand nights have brushed their balmy wings
Over these eyes; but ever when they closed,
Your tyrant image forced them ope again,
And dried the dews they brought:
The long expected hour is come at length,
By manly vengeance to redeem my fame;
And, that once cleared, eternal sleep is welcome.

SEBASTIAN
I have not yet forgot I am a king,
Whose royal office is redress of wrongs:
If I have wronged thee, charge me face to face;—
I have not yet forgot I am a soldier.

DORAX
'Tis the first justice thou hast ever done me.
Then, though I loath this woman's war of tongues,
Yet shall my cause of vengeance first be clear;
And, honour, be thou judge.

SEBASTIAN
Honour befriend us both.—
Beware I warn thee yet, to tell thy griefs
In terms becoming majesty to hear:
I warn thee thus, because I know thy temper
Is insolent, and haughty to superiors.
How often hast thou braved my peaceful court,
Filled it with noisy brawls, and windy boasts;
And with past service, nauseously repeated,
Reproached even me, thy prince?

DORAX
And well I might, when you forgot reward,
The part of heaven in kings; for punishment
Is hangman's work, and drudgery for devils.—
I must, and will reproach thee with my service,
Tyrant!—It irks me so to call my prince;
But just resentment, and hard usage, coined
The unwilling word; and, grating as it is,
Take it, for 'tis thy due.

SEBASTIAN
How, tyrant?

DORAX
Tyrant.

SEBASTIAN

Traitor!—that name thou canst not echo back;
That robe of infamy, that circumcision
Ill hid beneath that robe, proclaim thee traitor;
And, if a name
More foul than traitor be, 'tis renegade.

DORAX
If I'm a traitor, think,—and blush, thou tyrant,—
Whose injuries betrayed me into treason,
Effaced my loyalty, unhinged my faith,
And hurried me, from hopes of heaven, to hell.
All these, and all my yet unfinished crimes,
When I shall rise to plead before the saints,
I charge on thee, to make thy damning sure.

SEBASTIAN
Thy old presumptuous arrogance again,
That bred my first dislike, and then my loathing.—
Once more be warned, and know me for thy king.

DORAX
Too well I know thee, but for king no more.
This is not Lisbon; nor the circle this,
Where, like a statue, thou hast stood besieged
By sycophants and fools, the growth of courts;
Where thy gulled eyes, in all the gaudy round,
Met nothing but a lie in every face,
And the gross flattery of a gaping crowd,
Envious who first should catch, and first applaud,
The stuff of royal nonsense: When I spoke,
My honest homely words were carped and censured
For want of courtly style; related actions,
Though modestly reported, passed for boasts;
Secure of merit if I asked reward,
Thy hungry minions thought their rights invaded,
And the bread snatched from pimps and parasites.
Henriquez answered, with a ready lie,
To save his king's,—the boon was begged before!

SEBASTIAN
What say'st thou of Henriquez? Now, by heaven,
Thou mov'st me more by barely naming him,
Than all thy foul unmannered scurril taunts.

DORAX
And therefore 'twas, to gall thee, that I named him.
That thing, that nothing, but a cringe and smile;
That woman, but more daubed; or, if a man,

Corrupted to a woman; thy man-mistress.

SEBASTIAN
All false as hell, or thou.

DORAX
Yes; full as false
As that I served thee fifteen hard campaigns,
And pitched thy standard in these foreign fields:
By me thy greatness grew, thy years grew with it,
But thy ingratitude outgrew them both.

SEBASTIAN
I see to what thou tend'st: but, tell me first,
If those great acts were done alone for me?
If love produced not some, and pride the rest?

DORAX
Why, love does all that's noble here below;
But all the advantage of that love was thine.
For, coming fraughted back, in either hand
With palm and olive, victory and peace,
I was indeed prepared to ask my own,
(For Violante's vows were mine before:)
Thy malice had prevention, ere I spoke;
And asked me Violante for Henriquez.

SEBASTIAN
I meant thee a reward of greater worth.

DORAX
Where justice wanted, could reward be hoped?
Could the robbed passenger expect a bounty
From those rapacious hands, who stripped him first?

SEBASTIAN
He had my promise, ere I knew thy love.

DORAX
My services deserved thou shouldst revoke it.

SEBASTIAN
Thy insolence had cancelled all thy service:
To violate my laws, even in my court,
Sacred to peace, and safe from all affronts;
Even to my face, and done in my despite,
Under the wing of awful majesty,
To strike the man I loved!

DORAX
Even in the face of heaven, a place more sacred,
Would I have struck the man, who, prompt by power,
Would seize my right, and rob me of my love:
But, for a blow provoked by thy injustice,
The hasty product of a just despair,
When he refused to meet me in the field,
That thou shouldst make a coward's cause thy own!

SEBASTIAN
He durst; nay more, desired, and begged with tears,
To meet thy challenge fairly: 'Twas thy fault
To make it public; but my duty, then,
To interpose, on pain of my displeasure,
Betwixt your swords.

DORAX
On pain of infamy,
He should have disobeyed.

SEBASTIAN
The indignity, thou didst, was meant to me:
Thy gloomy eyes were cast on me with scorn,
As who should say,—the blow was there intended:
But that thou didst not dare to lift thy hands
Against anointed power. So was I forced
To do a sovereign justice to myself,
And spurn thee from my presence.

DORAX
Thou hast dared
To tell me, what I durst not tell myself:
I durst not think that I was spurned, and live;
And live to hear it boasted to my face.
All my long avarice of honour lost,
Heaped up in youth, and hoarded up for age!
Has honour's fountain then sucked back the stream?
He has; and hooting boys may dry-shod pass,
And gather pebbles from the naked ford.—
Give me my love, my honour; give them back—
Give me revenge, while I have breath to ask it!

SEBASTIAN
Now, by this honoured order which I wear,
More gladly would I give, than thou dar'st ask it;
Nor shall the sacred character of king
Be urged, to shield me from thy bold appeal.

If I have injured thee, that makes us equal;
The wrong, if done, debased me down to thee.
But thou hast charged me with ingratitude;
Hast thou not charged me? speak!

DORAX
Thou know'st I have:
If thou disown'st that imputation, draw,
And prove my charge a lie.

SEBASTIAN
No; to disprove that lie, I must not draw.
Be conscious to thy worth, and tell thy soul,
What thou hast done this day in my defence.
To fight thee after this, what were it else
Than owning that ingratitude thou urgest?
That isthmus stands between two rushing seas;
Which, mounting, view each other from afar,
And strive in vain to meet.

DORAX
I'll cut that isthmus.
Thou know'st I meant not to preserve thy life,
But to reprieve it, for my own revenge.
I saved thee out of honourable malice:
Now, draw;—I should be loth to think thou dar'st not:
Beware of such another vile excuse.

SEBASTIAN
O patience, heaven!

DORAX
Beware of patience, too;
That's a suspicious word. It had been proper,
Before thy foot had spurned me; now 'tis base:
Yet, to disarm thee of thy last defence,
I have thy oath for my security.
The only boon I begged was this fair combat:
Fight, or be perjured now; that's all thy choice.

SEBASTIAN
Now can I thank thee as thou would'st be thanked.

[Drawing.

Never was vow of honour better paid,
If my true sword but hold, than this shall be.
The sprightly bridegroom, on his wedding night,

More gladly enters not the lists of love:
Why, 'tis enjoyment to be summoned thus.
Go, bear my message to Henriquez ghost;
And say, his master and his friend revenged him.

DORAX
His ghost! then is my hated rival dead?

SEBASTIAN
The question is beside our present purpose:
Thou seest me ready; we delay too long.

DORAX
A minute is not much in either's life,
When there's but one betwixt us; throw it in,
And give it him of us who is to fail.

SEBASTIAN
He's dead; make haste, and thou may'st yet o'ertake him.

DORAX
When I was hasty, thou delayed'st me longer—
I pr'ythee let me hedge one moment more
Into thy promise: For thy life preserved,
Be kind; and tell me how that rival died,
Whose death, next thine, I wished.

SEBASTIAN
If it would please thee, thou shouldst never know;
But thou, like jealousy, enquir'st a truth,
Which, found, will torture thee.—He died in fight;
Fought next my person; as in concert fought;
Kept pace for pace, and blow for every blow;
Save when he heaved his shield in my defence,
And on his naked side received my wound.
Then, when he could no more, he fell at once;
But rolled his falling body cross their way,
And made a bulwark of it for his prince.

DORAX
I never can forgive him such a death!

SEBASTIAN
I prophesied thy proud soul could not bear it.—
Now, judge thyself, who best deserved my love?
I knew you both; and (durst I say) as heaven
Foreknew, among the shining angel host,
Who would stand firm, who fall.

DORAX
Had he been tempted so, so had he fallen;
And so had I been favoured, had I stood.

SEBASTIAN
What had been, is unknown; what is, appears.
Confess, he justly was preferred to thee.

DORAX
Had I been born with his indulgent stars,
My fortune had been his, and his been mine.—
O worse than hell! what glory have I lost,
And what has he acquired, by such a death!
I should have fallen by Sebastian's side,
My corps had been the bulwark of my king.
His glorious end was a patched work of fate,
Ill sorted with a soft effeminate life;
It suited better with my life than his,
So to have died: Mine had been of a piece,
Spent in your service, dying at your feet.

SEBASTIAN
The more effeminate and soft his life,
The more his fame, to struggle to the field,
And meet his glorious fate. Confess, proud spirit,
(For I will have it from thy very mouth)
That better he deserved my love than thou?

DORAX
O, whither would you drive me? I must grant,—
Yes, I must grant, but with a swelling soul,—
Henriquez had your love with more desert.
For you he fought, and died: I fought against you;
Through all the mazes of the bloody field,
Hunted your sacred life; which that I missed
Was the propitious error of my fate,
Not of my soul: My soul's a regicide.

SEBASTIAN [More calmly.]
Thou might'st have given it a more gentle name.
Thou meant'st to kill a tyrant, not a king:
Speak, didst thou not, Alonzo?

DORAX
Can I speak!
Alas, I cannot answer to Alonzo!—
No, Dorax cannot answer to Alonzo;

Alonzo was too kind a name for me.
Then, when I fought and conquered with your arms,
In that blest age, I was the man you named:
Till rage and pride debased me into Dorax,
And lost, like Lucifer, my name above.

SEBASTIAN
Yet twice this day I owed my life to Dorax.

DORAX
I saved you but to kill you: There's my grief.

SEBASTIAN
Nay, if thou can'st be grieved, thou can'st repent;
Thou could'st not be a villain, though thou would'st:
Thou own'st too much, in owning thou hast erred;
And I too little, who provoked thy crime.

DORAX
O stop this headlong torrent of your goodness!
It comes too fast upon a feeble soul,
Half drowned in tears before: Spare my confusion;
For pity spare; and say not first, you erred;
For yet I have not dared, through guilt and shame,
To throw myself beneath your royal feet.—

[Falls at his feet.

Now spurn this rebel, this proud renegade;
'Tis just you should, nor will I more complain.

SEBASTIAN
Indeed thou should'st not ask forgiveness first;
But thou prevent'st me still, in all that's noble.

[Taking him up.

Yes, I will raise thee up with better news.
Thy Violante's heart was ever thine;
Compelled to wed, because she was my ward,
Her soul was absent when she gave her hand;
Nor could my threats, or his pursuing courtship,
Effect the consummation of his love:
So, still indulging tears, she pines for thee,
A widow, and a maid.

DORAX
Have I been cursing heaven, while heaven blest me?

I shall run mad with extacy of joy:
What! in one moment, to be reconciled
To heaven, and to my king, and to my love!—
But pity is my friend, and stops me short,
For my unhappy rival:—Poor Henriquez!

SEBASTIAN
Art thou so generous, too, to pity him?
Nay, then, I was unjust to love him better.
Here let me ever hold thee in my arms;

[Embracing him.

And all our quarrels be but such as these,
Who shall love best, and closest shall embrace.
Be what Henriquez was,—be my Alonzo.

DORAX
What, my Alonzo, said you? my Alonzo!
Let my tears thank you, for I cannot speak;
And, if I could,
Words were not made to vent such thoughts as mine.

SEBASTIAN
Some strange reverse of fate must sure attend
This vast profusion, this extravagance
Of heaven, to bless me thus. 'Tis gold so pure,
It cannot bear the stamp, without alloy.—
Be kind, ye powers! and take but half away:
With ease the gifts of fortune I resign;
But let my love and friend be ever mine.

[Exeunt.

ACT V

SCENE I

The Scene is a Room of State

Enter **DORAX** and **ANTONIO**.

DORAX
Joy is on every face, without a cloud;
As, in the scene of opening paradise,
The whole creation danced at their new being,

Pleased to be what they were, pleased with each other,
Such joy have I, both in myself and friends;
And double joy that I have made them happy.

ANTONIO
Pleasure has been the business of my life;
And every change of fortune easy to me,
Because I still was easy to myself.
The loss of her I loved would touch me nearest;
Yet, if I found her, I might love too much,
And that's uneasy pleasure.

DORAX
If she be fated
To be your wife, your fate will find her for you:
Predestinated ills are never lost.

ANTONIO
I had forgot
To inquire before, but long to be informed,
How, poisoned and betrayed, and round beset,
You could unwind yourself from all these dangers,
And move so speedily to our relief?

DORAX
The double poisons, after a short combat,
Expelled each other in their civil war,
By nature's benefit, and roused my thoughts
To guard that life which now I found attacked.
I summoned all my officers in haste,
On whose experienced faith I might rely;
All came resolved to die in my defence,
Save that one villain who betrayed the gate.
Our diligence prevented the surprise
We justly feared: So Muley-Zeydan found us
Drawn up in battle, to receive the charge.

ANTONIO
But how the Moors and Christian slaves were joined,
You have not yet unfolded.

DORAX
That remains.
We knew their interest was the same with ours:
And, though I hated more than death Sebastian,
I could not see him die by vulgar hands;
But, prompted by my angel, or by his,
Freed all the slaves, and placed him next myself,

Because I would not have his person known.
I need not tell the rest, the event declares it.

ANTONIO
Your conquests came of course; their men were raw,
And yours were disciplined.—One doubt remains,
Why you industriously concealed the king,
Who, known, had added courage to his men?

DORAX
I would not hazard civil broils betwixt
His friends and mine; which might prevent our combat.
Yet, had he fallen, I had dismissed his troops;
Or, if victorious, ordered his escape.—
But I forgot a new increase of joy
To feast him with surprise; I must about it:
Expect my swift return.

[Exit.

[Enter a **SERVANT**.

SERVANT
Here's a lady at the door, that bids me tell you, she is come to make an end of the game, that was broken off betwixt you.

ANTONIO
What manner of woman is she? Does she not want two of the four elements? has she any thing about her but air and fire?

SERVANT
Truly, she flies about the room as if she had wings instead of legs; I believe she's just turning into a bird:—A house bird I warrant her:—And so hasty to fly to you, that, rather than fail of entrance, she would come tumbling down the chimney, like a swallow.

[Enter **MORAYMA**.

ANTONIO [Running to her, and embracing her.]
Look, if she be not here already!—What, no denial it seems will serve your turn? Why, thou little dun, is thy debt so pressing?

MORAYMA
Little devil, if you please: Your lease is out, good master conjurer, and I am come to fetch your soul and body; not an hour of lewdness longer in this world for you.

ANTONIO
Where the devil hast thou been? and how the devil didst thou find me here?

MORAYMA
I followed you into the castle-yard, but there was nothing but tumult and confusion: and I was bodily afraid of being picked up by some of the rabble; considering I had a double charge about me,—my jewels, and my maidenhead.

ANTONIO
Both of them intended for my worship's sole use and property.

MORAYMA
And what was poor little I among them all?

ANTONIO
Not a mouthful a-piece: 'Twas too much odds, in conscience!

MORAYMA
So, seeking for shelter, I naturally ran to the old place of assignation, the garden-house; where, for the want of instinct, you did not follow me.

ANTONIO
Well, for thy comfort, I have secured thy father; and I hope thou hast secured his effects for us.

MORAYMA
Yes, truly, I had the prudent foresight to consider, that, when we grow old, and weary of solacing one another, we might have, at least, wherewithal to make merry with the world; and take up with a worse pleasure of eating and drinking, when we were disabled for a better.

ANTONIO
Thy fortune will be even too good for thee; for thou art going into the country of serenades and gallantries, where thy street will be haunted every night with thy foolish lovers, and my rivals, who will be sighing and singing, under thy inexorable windows, lamentable ditties, and call thee cruel, and goddess, and moon, and stars, and all the poetical names of wicked rhime; while thou and I are minding our business, and jogging on, and laughing at them, at leisure minutes, which will be very few; take that by way of threatening.

MORAYMA
I am afraid you are not very valiant, that you huff so much beforehand. But, they say, your churches are fine places for love-devotion; many a she-saint is there worshipped.

ANTONIO
Temples are there, as they are in all other countries, good conveniences for dumb interviews. I hear the protestants are not much reformed in that point neither; for their sectaries call their churches by the natural name of meeting-houses. Therefore I warn thee in good time, not more of devotion than needs must, good future spouse, and always in a veil; for those eyes of thine are damned enemies to mortification.

MORAYMA

The best thing I have heard of Christendom is, that we women are allowed the privilege of having souls; and I assure you, I shall make bold to bestow mine upon some lover, whenever you begin to go astray; and, if I find no convenience in a church, a private chamber will serve the turn.

ANTONIO
When that day comes, I must take my revenge, and turn gardener again; for I find I am much given to planting.

MORAYMA
But take heed, in the mean time, that some young Antonio does not spring up in your own family; as false as his father, though of another man's planting.

[Re-enter **DORAX**, with **SEBASTIAN** and **ALMEYDA**, **SEBASTIAN** enters speaking to **DORAX**, while in the mean time **ANTONIO** presents **MORAYMA** to **ALMEYDA**.

SEBASTIAN
How fares our royal prisoner, Muley-Zeydan?

DORAX
Disposed to grant whatever I desire,
To gain a crown, and freedom. Well I know him,
Of easy temper, naturally good,
And faithful to his word.

SEBASTIAN
Yet one thing wants,
To fill the measure of my happiness;
I'm still in pain for poor Alvarez' life.

DORAX
Release that fear, the good old man is safe;
I paid his ransom,
And have already ordered his attendance.

SEBASTIAN
O bid him enter, for I long to see him.

[Enter **ALVAREZ** with a **SERVANT**, who departs when **ALVAREZ** is entered.

ALVAREZ
Now by my soul, and by these hoary hairs,

[Falling down, and embracing the **KING'S** knees.

I'm so o'erwhelmed with pleasure, that I feel
A latter spring within my withering limbs,
That shoots me out again.

SEBASTIAN
Thou good old man,

[Raising him.

Thou hast deceived me into more, more joys,
Who stood brim-full before.

ALVAREZ
O my dear child,—
I love thee so, I cannot call thee king,—
Whom I so oft have dandled in these arms!
What, when I gave thee lost, to find thee living!
'Tis like a father, who himself had 'scaped
A falling house, and, after anxious search,
Hears from afar his only son within;
And digs through rubbish, till he drags him out,
To see the friendly light.
Such is my haste, so trembling is my joy,
To draw thee forth from underneath thy fate.

SEBASTIAN
The tempest is o'erblown, the skies are clear,
And the sea charmed into a calm so still,
That not a wrinkle ruffles her smooth face.

ALVAREZ
Just such she shows before a rising storm;
And therefore am I come with timely speed,
To warn you into port.

ALMEYDA
My soul forebodes
Some dire event involved in those dark words,
And just disclosing in a birth of fate. [Aside.

ALVAREZ
Is there not yet an heir of this vast empire,
Who still survives, of Muley-Moluch's branch?

DORAX
Yes, such a one there is a captive here,
And brother to the dead.

ALVAREZ
The powers above
Be praised for that! My prayers for my good master,
I hope, are heard.

SEBASTIAN
Thou hast a right in heaven.
But why these prayers for me?

ALVAREZ
A door is open yet for your deliverance.—
Now you, my countrymen, and you, Almeyda,
Now all of us, and you, my all in one,
May yet be happy in that captive's life.

SEBASTIAN
We have him here an honourable hostage
For terms of peace; what more he can contribute
To make me blest, I know not.

ALVAREZ
Vastly more;
Almeyda may be settled in the throne,
And you review your native clime with fame.
A firm alliance and eternal peace,
The glorious crown of honourable war,
Are all included in that prince's life.
Let this fair queen be given to Muley-Zeydan,
And make her love the sanction of your league.

SEBASTIAN
No more of that; his life's in my dispose,
And prisoners are not to insist on terms;
Or, if they were, yet he demands not these.

ALVAREZ
You should exact them.

ALMEYDA
Better may be made,
These cannot: I abhor the tyrant's race,—
My parents' murderers, my throne's usurpers.
But, at one blow, to cut off all dispute,
Know this, thou busy, old, officious man,—
I am a Christian; now be wise no more;
Or, if thou wouldst be still thought wise, be silent.

ALVAREZ
O, I perceive you think your interest touched:
'Tis what before the battle I observed;
But I must speak, and will.

SEBASTIAN
I pr'ythee, peace;
Perhaps she thinks they are too near of blood.

ALVAREZ
I wish she may not wed to blood more near.

SEBASTIAN
What if I make her mine?

ALVAREZ
Now heaven forbid!

SEBASTIAN
Wish rather heaven may grant;
For, if I could deserve, I have deserved her:
My toils, my hazards, and my subjects' lives,
Provided she consent, may claim her love;
And, that once granted, I appeal to these,
If better I could chuse a beauteous bride.

ANTONIO
The fairest of her sex.

MORAYMA
The pride of nature.

DORAX
He only merits her, she only him;
So paired, so suited in their minds and persons,
That they were framed the tallies for each other.
If any alien love had interposed,
It must have been an eye-sore to beholders,
And to themselves a curse.

ALVAREZ
And to themselves
The greatest curse that can be, were to join.

SEBASTIAN
Did not I love thee past a change to hate,
That word had been thy ruin; but no more,
I charge thee, on thy life, perverse old man!

ALVAREZ
Know, sir, I would be silent if I durst:
But if, on shipboard, I should see my friend
Grown frantic in a raging calenture,

And he, imagining vain flowery fields,
Would headlong plunge himself into the deep,—
Should I not hold him from that mad attempt,
Till his sick fancy were by reason cured?

SEBASTIAN
I pardon thee the effects of doting age,
Vain doubts, and idle cares, and over-caution;
The second nonage of a soul more wise,
But now decayed, and sunk into the socket;
Peeping by fits, and giving feeble light.

ALVAREZ
Have you forgot?

SEBASTIAN
Thou mean'st my father's will,
In bar of marriage to Almeyda's bed.
Thou seest my faculties are still entire,
Though thine are much impaired. I weighed that will,
And found 'twas grounded on our different faiths;
But, had he lived to see her happy change,
He would have cancelled that harsh interdict,
And joined our hands himself.

ALVAREZ
Still had he lived and seen this change,
He still had been the same.

SEBASTIAN
I have a dark remembrance of my father:
His reasonings and his actions both were just;
And, granting that, he must have changed his measures.

ALVAREZ
Yes, he was just, and therefore could not change.

SEBASTIAN
'Tis a base wrong thou offer'st to the dead.

ALVAREZ
Now heaven forbid,
That I should blast his pious memory!
No, I am tender of his holy fame;
For, dying, he bequeathed it to my charge.
Believe, I am; and seek to know no more,
But pay a blind obedience to his will;
For, to preserve his fame, I would be silent.

SEBASTIAN
Crazed fool, who would'st be thought an oracle,
Come down from off the tripos, and speak plain.
My father shall be justified, he shall:
'Tis a son's part to rise in his defence,
And to confound thy malice, or thy dotage.

ALVAREZ
It does not grieve me, that you hold me crazed;
But, to be cleared at my dead master's cost,
O there's the wound! but let me first adjure you,
By all you owe that dear departed soul,
No more to think of marriage with Almeyda.

SEBASTIAN
Not heaven and earth combined can hinder it.

ALVAREZ
Then witness heaven and earth, how loth I am
To say, you must not, nay, you cannot, wed:
And since not only a dead father's fame,
But more, a lady's honour, must be touched,
Which, nice as ermines, will not bear a soil,
Let all retire, that you alone may hear
What even in whispers I would tell your ear.

[All are going out.

ALMEYDA
Not one of you depart; I charge you, stay!
And were my voice a trumpet loud as fame,
To reach the round of heaven, and earth, and sea,
All nations should be summoned to this place,
So little do I fear that fellow's charge:
So should my honour, like a rising swan,
Brush with her wings the falling drops away,
And proudly plough the waves.

SEBASTIAN
This noble pride becomes thy innocence;
And I dare trust my father's memory,
To stand the charge of that foul forging tongue.

ALVAREZ
It will be soon discovered if I forge.
Have you not heard your father in his youth,
When newly married, travelled into Spain,

And made a long abode in Philip's court?

SEBASTIAN
Why so remote a question, which thyself
Can answer to thyself? for thou wert with him,
His favourite, as I oft have heard thee boast,
And nearest to his soul.

ALVAREZ
Too near, indeed; forgive me, gracious heaven,
That ever I should boast I was so near,
The confident of all his young amours!—
And have not you, unhappy beauty, heard, [To **ALMEYDA**.
Have you not often heard, your exiled parents
Were refuged in that court, and at that time?

ALMEYDA
'Tis true; and often since my mother owned,
How kind that prince was to espouse her cause;
She counselled, nay enjoined me on her blessing,
To seek the sanctuary of your court;
Which gave me first encouragement to come,
And, with my brother, beg Sebastian's aid.

SEBASTIAN
Thou helpst me well to justify my war:
[To **ALMEYDA**] My dying father swore me, then a boy,
And made me kiss the cross upon his sword,
Never to sheath it, till that exiled queen
Were by my arms restored.

ALMEYDA
And can you find
No mystery couched in this excess of kindness?
Were kings e'er known, in this degenerate age,
So passionately fond of noble acts,
Where interest shared not more than half with honour?

SEBASTIAN
Base grovelling soul, who know'st not honour's worth,
But weigh'st it out in mercenary scales!
The secret pleasure of a generous act
Is the great mind's great bribe.

ALVAREZ
Show me that king, and I'll believe the Phoenix.
But knock at your own breast, and ask your soul,
If those fair fatal eyes edged not your sword

More than your father's charge, and all your vows?
If so,—and so your silence grants it is,—
Know king, your father had, like you, a soul,
And love is your inheritance from him.
Almeyda's mother, too, had eyes, like her,
And not less charming; and were charmed no less
Than yours are now with her, and hers with you.

ALMEYDA
Thou liest, impostor! perjured fiend, thou liest!

SEBASTIAN
Was't not enough to brand my father's fame,
But thou must load a lady's memory?
O infamous! O base, beyond repair!
And to what end this ill-concerted lie,
Which palpable and gross, yet granted true,
It bars not my inviolable vows?

ALVAREZ
Take heed, and double not your father's crimes;
To his adultery do not add your incest.
Know, she's the product of unlawful love,
And 'tis your carnal sister you would wed.

SEBASTIAN
Thou shalt not say thou wer't condemned unheard;
Else, by my soul, this moment were thy last.

ALMEYDA
But think not oaths shall justify thy charge,
Nor imprecations on thy cursed head;
For who dares lie to heaven, thinks heaven a jest.
Thou hast confessed thyself the conscious pandar
Of that pretended passion;
A single witness infamously known,
Against two persons of unquestioned fame.

ALVAREZ
What interest can I have, or what delight,
To blaze their shame, or to divulge my own?
If proved, you hate me; if unproved, condemn.
Not racks or tortures could have forced this secret,
But too much care to save you from a crime,
Which would have sunk you both. For, let me say,
Almeyda's beauty well deserves your love.

ALMEYDA

Out, base impostor! I abhor thy praise.

DORAX
It looks not like imposture; but a truth,
On utmost need revealed.

SEBASTIAN
Did I expect from Dorax this return?
Is this the love renewed?

DORAX
Sir, I am silent;
Pray heaven my fears prove false!

SEBASTIAN
Away! you all combine to make me wretched.

ALVAREZ
But hear the story of that fatal love,
Where every circumstance shall prove another;
And truth so shine by her own native light,
That, if a lie were mixt, it must be seen.

SEBASTIAN
No; all may still be forged, and of a piece.
No; I can credit nothing thou canst say.

ALVAREZ
One proof remains, and that's your father's hand,
Firmed with his signet; both so fully known,
That plainer evidence can hardly be,
Unless his soul would want her heaven awhile,
And come on earth to swear.

SEBASTIAN
Produce that writing.

ALVAREZ [To **DORAX**.]
Alonzo has it in his custody;
The same, which, when his nobleness redeemed me,
And in a friendly visit owned himself
For what he is, I then deposited,
And had his faith to give it to the king.

DORAX
Untouched, and sealed, as when intrusted with me,

[Giving a sealed Paper to the **KING**.

Such I restore it with a trembling hand,
Lest aught within disturb your peace of soul.

SEBASTIAN
Draw near, Almeyda; thou art most concerned,
For I am most in thee.—

[Tearing open the Seals.

Alonzo, mark the characters;
Thou know'st my father's hand, observe it well;
And if the impostor's pen have made one slip
That shews it counterfeit, mark that, and save me.

DORAX
It looks indeed too like my master's hand:
So does the signet: more I cannot say;
But wish 'twere not so like.

SEBASTIAN
Methinks it owns
The black adultery, and Almeyda's birth;
But such a mist of grief comes o'er my eyes,
I cannot, or I would not, read it plain.

ALMEYDA
Heaven cannot be more true, than this is false.

SEBASTIAN
O couldst thou prove it with the same assurance!
Speak, hast thou ever seen my father's hand?

ALMEYDA
No; but my mother's honour has been read
By me, and by the world, in all her acts,
In characters more plain and legible
Than this dumb evidence, this blotted lie.—
Oh that I were a man, as my soul's one,
To prove thee traitor, and assassinate
Of her fame! thus moved, I'd tear thee thus,—

[Tearing the Paper.

And scatter o'er the field thy coward limbs,
Like this foul offspring of thy forging brain.

[Scattering the Paper.

ALVAREZ
Just so shalt thou be torn from all thy hopes;
For know, proud woman, know, in thy despite,
The most authentic proof is still behind,—
Thou wear'st it on thy finger: 'Tis that ring,
Which, matched to that on his, shall clear the doubt.
'Tis no dumb forgery, for that shall speak,
And sound a rattling peal to either's conscience.

SEBASTIAN
This ring, indeed, my father, with a cold
And shaking hand, just in the pangs of death,
Put on my finger, with a parting sigh;
And would have, spoke, but faultered in his speech,
With undistinguished sound.

ALVAREZ
I know it well,
For I was present.—Now, Almeyda, speak,
And truly tell us how you came by yours.

ALMEYDA
My mother, when I parted from her sight
To go to Portugal, bequeathed it to me,
Presaging she should never see me more.
She pulled it from her finger, shed some tears,
Kissed it, and told me 'twas a pledge of love,
And hid a mystery of great importance,
Relating to my fortunes.

ALVAREZ
Mark me now,
While I disclose that fatal mystery:—
Those rings, when you were born and thought another's,
Your parents, glowing yet in sinful love,
Bid me bespeak: a curious artist wrought them.
With joints so close, as not to be perceived,
Yet are they both each other's counterpart;
Her part had Juan inscribed, and his had Zayda,
(You know those names are theirs,) and in the midst
A heart divided in two halves was placed.
Now, if the rivets of those rings inclosed
Fit not each other, I have forged this lie;
But, if they join, you must for ever part.

[**SEBASTIAN** pulling off his Ring, **ALMEYDA** does the same, and gives it to **ALVAREZ**, who unscrews both the Rings, and fits one half to the other[10].

SEBASTIAN
Now life, or death.

ALMEYDA
And either thine, or ours.—
I'm lost for ever.

[Swoons. The **WOMEN** and **MORAYMA** take her up, and carry her off. **SEBASTIAN** here stands amazed without motion, his eyes fixed upward.

SEBASTIAN
Look to the queen, my wife; for I am past
All power of aid to her, or to myself.

ALVAREZ
His wife! said he, his wife! O fatal sound!
For, had I known it, this unwelcome news
Had never reached their ears:
So they had still been blest in ignorance,
And I alone unhappy.

DORAX
I knew it, but too late, and durst not speak.

SEBASTIAN
[Starting out of his amazement.]
I will not live, no not a moment more;
I will not add one moment more to incest;
I'll cut it off, and end a wretched being:
For, should I live, my soul's so little mine,
And so much hers, that I should still enjoy.—
Ye cruel powers,
Take me, as you have made me, miserable;
You cannot make me guilty; 'twas my fate,
And you made that, not I.

[Draws his Sword. **ANTONIO** and **ALVAREZ** lay hold on him, and **DORAX** wrests the Sword out of his hand.

ANTONIO
For heaven's sake hold, and recollect your mind!

ALVAREZ
Consider whom you punish, and for what;
Yourself unjustly; you have charged the fault
On heaven, that best may bear it.
Though incest is indeed a deadly crime,

You are not guilty, since unknown 'twas done,
And, known, had been abhorred.

SEBASTIAN
By heaven, you're traitors all, that hold my hands.
If death be but cessation of our thought,
Then let me die, for I would think no more.
I'll boast my innocence above,
And let them see a soul they could not sully,
I shall be there before my father's ghost,
That yet must languish long in frosts and fires,
For making me unhappy by his crime.—
Stand oft, and let me take my fill of death;

[Struggling again.

For I can hold my breath in your despite,
And swell my heaving soul out when I please.

ALVAREZ
Heaven comfort you!

SEBASTIAN
What, art thou giving comfort!
Wouldst thou give comfort, who hast given despair?
Thou seest Alonzo silent; he's a man.
He knows, that men, abandoned of their hopes,
Should ask no leave, nor stay for sueing out
A tedious writ of ease from lingering heaven,
But help themselves as timely as they could,
And teach the Fates their duty.

DORAX [To **ALVAREZ** and **ANTONIO**]
Let him go;
He is our king, and he shall be obeyed.

ALVAREZ
What, to destroy himself? O parricide!

DORAX
Be not injurious in your foolish zeal,
But leave him free; or, by my sword, I swear
To hew that arm away, that stops the passage
To his eternal rest.

ANTONIO [Letting go his hold.]
Let him be guilty of his own death, if
he pleases; for I'll not be guilty of mine, by holding him.

[The **KING** shakes off **ALVAREZ**.

ALVAREZ [To **DORAX**]
Infernal fiend,
Is this a subject's part?

DORAX
'Tis a friend's office.
He has convinced me, that he ought to die;
And, rather than he should not, here's my sword,
To help him on his journey.

SEBASTIAN
My last, my only friend, how kind art thou,
And how inhuman these!

DORAX
To make the trifle, death, a thing of moment!

SEBASTIAN
And not to weigh the important cause I had
To rid myself of life!

DORAX
True; for a crime
So horrid, in the face of men and angels,
As wilful incest is!

SEBASTIAN
Not wilful, neither.

DORAX
Yes, if you lived, and with repeated acts
Refreshed your sin, and loaded crimes with crimes,
To swell your scores of guilt.

SEBASTIAN
True; if I lived.

DORAX
I said so, if you lived.

SEBASTIAN
For hitherto was fatal ignorance,
And no intended crime.

DORAX

That you best know;
But the malicious world will judge the worst.

ALVAREZ
O what a sophister has hell procured,
To argue for damnation!

DORAX
Peace, old dotard.
Mankind, that always judge of kings with malice,
Will think he knew this incest, and pursued it.
His only way to rectify mistakes,
And to redeem her honour, is to die.

SEBASTIAN
Thou hast it right, my dear, my best Alonzo!
And that, but petty reparation too;
But all I have to give.

DORAX
Your, pardon, sir;
You may do more, and ought.

SEBASTIAN
What, more than death?

DORAX
Death! why, that's children's sport; a stage-play death;
We act it every night we go to bed.
Death, to a man in misery, is sleep.
Would you,—who perpetrated such a crime,
As frightened nature, made the saints above
Shake heavens eternal pavement with their trembling
To view that act,—would you but barely die?
But stretch your limbs, and turn on t'other side.
To lengthen out a black voluptuous slumber,
And dream you had your sister in your arms?

SEBASTIAN
To expiate this, can I do more than die?

DORAX
O yes, you must do more, you must be damned;
You must be damned to all eternity;
And sure self-murder is the readiest way.

SEBASTIAN
How, damned?

DORAX
Why, is that news?

ALVAREZ
O horror, horror!

DORAX
What, thou a statesman,
And make a business of damnation
In such a world as this! why, 'tis a trade;
The scrivener, usurer, lawyer, shopkeeper,
And soldier, cannot live but by damnation.
The politician does it by advance,
And gives all gone beforehand.

SEBASTIAN
O thou hast given me such a glimpse of hell,
So pushed me forward, even to the brink
Of that irremeable burning gulph,
That, looking in the abyss, I dare not leap.
And now I see what good thou mean'st my soul,
And thank thy pious fraud; thou hast indeed
Appeared a devil, but didst an angel's work.

DORAX
'Twas the last remedy, to give you leisure;
For, if you could but think, I knew you safe.

SEBASTIAN
I thank thee, my Alonzo; I will live,
But never more to Portugal return;
For, to go back and reign, that were to show
Triumphant incest, and pollute the throne.

ALVAREZ
Since ignorance—

SEBASTIAN
O, palliate not my wound;
When you have argued all you can, 'tis incest.
No, 'tis resolved: I charge you plead no more;
I cannot live without Almeyda's sight,
Nor can I see Almeyda, but I sin.
Heaven has inspired me with a sacred thought,
To live alone to heaven, and die to her.

DORAX

Mean you to turn an anchorite?

SEBASTIAN
What else?
The world was once too narrow for my mind,
But one poor little nook will serve me now,
To hide me from the rest of human kind.
Africk has deserts wide enough to hold
Millions of monsters; and I am, sure, the greatest.

ALVAREZ
You may repent, and wish your crown too late.

SEBASTIAN
O never, never; I am past a boy:
A sceptre's but a plaything, and a globe
A bigger bounding stone. He, who can leave
Almeyda, may renounce the rest with ease.

DORAX
O truly great!
A soul fixed high, and capable of heaven.
Old as he is, your uncle cardinal
Is not so far enamoured of a cloister,
But he will thank you for the crown you leave him.

SEBASTIAN
To please him more, let him believe me dead,
That he may never dream I may return.
Alonzo, I am now no more thy king,
But still thy friend; and by that holy name
Adjure thee, to perform my last request;—
Make our conditions with yon captive king;
Secure me but my solitary cell;
'Tis all I ask him for a crown restored.

DORAX
I will do more:
But fear not Muley-Zeydan; his soft metal
Melts down with easy warmth, runs in the mould,
And needs no further forge.

[Exit **DORAX**.

[Re-enter **ALMEYDA** led by **MORAYMA**, and followed by her **ATTENDANTS**.

SEBASTIAN
See where she comes again!

By heaven, when I behold those beauteous eyes,
Repentance lags, and sin comes hurrying on.

ALMEYDA
This is too cruel!

SEBASTIAN
Speak'st thou of love, of fortune, or of death,
Or double death? for we must part, Almeyda.

ALMEYDA
I speak of all,
For all things that belong to us are cruel;
But, what's most cruel, we must love no more.
O 'tis too much that I must never see you,
But not to love you is impossible.
No, I must love you; heaven may bate me that,
And charge that sinful sympathy of souls
Upon our parents, when they loved too well.

SEBASTIAN
Good heaven, thou speak'st my thoughts, and I speak thine!
Nay, then there's incest in our very souls,
For we were formed too like.

ALMEYDA
Too like indeed,
And yet not for each other.
Sure when we part, (for I resolved it too,
Though you proposed it first,) however distant,
We shall be ever thinking of each other,
And the same moment for each other pray.

SEBASTIAN
But if a wish should come athwart our prayers!

ALMEYDA
It would do well to curb it, if we could.

SEBASTIAN
We cannot look upon each other's face,
But, when we read our love, we read our guilt:
And yet, methinks, I cannot chuse but love.

ALMEYDA
I would have asked you, if I durst for shame,
If still you loved? you gave it air before me.
Ah, why were we not born both of a sex?

For then we might have loved without a crime.
Why was not I your brother? though that wish
Involved our parents' guilt, we had not parted;
We had been friends, and friendship is no incest.

SEBASTIAN
Alas, I know not by what name to call thee!
Sister and wife are the two dearest names,
And I would call thee both, and both are sin.
Unhappy we! that still we must confound
The dearest names into a common curse.

ALMEYDA
To love, and be beloved, and yet be wretched!

SEBASTIAN
To have but one poor night of all our lives;
It was indeed a glorious, guilty night;
So happy, that—forgive me, heaven!—I wish,
With all its guilt, it were to come again.
Why did we know so soon, or why at all,
That sin could be concealed in such a bliss?

ALMEYDA
Men have a larger privilege of words,
Else I should speak; but we must part, Sebastian,—
That's all the name that I have left to call thee;—
I must not call thee by the name I would;
But when I say Sebastian, dear Sebastian,
I kiss the name I speak.

SEBASTIAN
We must make haste, or we shall never part.
I would say something that's as dear as this;
Nay, would do more than say: One moment longer,
And I should break through laws divine and human,
And think them cobwebs spread for little man,
Which all the bulky herd of nature breaks.
The vigorous young world was ignorant
Of these restrictions; 'tis decrepit now;
Not more devout, but more decayed, and cold.—
All this is impious, therefore we must part;
For, gazing thus, I kindle at thy sight,
And, once burnt down to tinder, light again
Much sooner than before.

[Re-enter **DORAX**.

ALMEYDA
Here comes the sad denouncer of my fate,
To toll the mournful knell of separation;
While I, as on my deathbed, hear the sound,
That warns me hence for ever.

SEBASTIAN [To **DORAX**]
Now be brief,
And I will try to listen,
And share the minute, that remains, betwixt
The care I owe my subjects, and my love.

DORAX
Your fate has gratified you all she can;
Gives easy misery, and makes exile pleasing.
I trusted Muley-Zeydan as a friend,
But swore him first to secrecy: He wept
Your fortune, and with tears not squeezed by art,
But shed from nature, like a kindly shower:
In short, he proffered more than I demanded;
A safe retreat, a gentle solitude,
Unvexed with noise, and undisturbed with fears.
I chose you one—

ALMEYDA
O do not tell me where;
For, if I knew the place of his abode,
I should be tempted to pursue his steps,
And then we both were lost.

SEBASTIAN
Even past redemption;
For, if I knew thou wert on that design,
(As I must know, because our souls are one,)
I should not wander, but by sure instinct
Should meet thee just half-way in pilgrimage,
And close for ever; for I know my love
More strong than thine, and I more frail than thou.

ALMEYDA
Tell me not that; for I must boast my crime,
And cannot bear that thou should'st better love.

DORAX
I may inform you both; for you must go,
Where seas, and winds, and deserts will divide you.
Under the ledge of Atlas lies a cave,
Cut in the living rock by Nature's hands,

The venerable seat of holy hermits;
Who there, secure in separated cells,
Sacred even to the Moors, enjoy devotion;
And from the purling streams, and savage fruits.
Have wholesome beverage, and unbloody feasts.

SEBASTIAN
'Tis penance too voluptuous for my crime[11].

DORAX
Your subjects, conscious of your life, are few;
But all desirous to partake your exile,
And to do office to your sacred person.
The rest, who think you dead, shall be dismissed.
Under safe convoy, till they reach your fleet.

ALMEYDA
But how am wretched I to be disposed?—
A vain enquiry, since I leave my lord;
For all the world beside is banishment.

DORAX
I have a sister, abbess in Terceras,
Who lost her lover on her bridal day.

ALMEYDA
There fate provided me a fellow-turtle,
To mingle sighs with sighs, and tears with tears.

DORAX
Last, for myself, if I have well fulfilled
My sad commission, let me beg the boon,
To share the sorrows of your last recess,
And mourn the common losses of our loves.

ALVAREZ
And what becomes of me? must I be left,
As age and time had worn me out of use?
These sinews are not yet so much unstrung,
To fail me when my master should be served;
And when they are, then will I steal to death,
Silent and unobserved, to save his tears.

SEBASTIAN
I've heard you both;—Alvarez, have thy wish;—
But thine, Alonzo, thine is too unjust.
I charge thee with my last commands, return,
And bless thy Violante with thy vows.—

Antonio, be thou happy too in thine.
Last, let me swear you all to secrecy;
And, to conceal my shame, conceal my life.

DORAX, ANTONIO, MORAYMA
We swear to keep it secret.

ALMEYDA
Now I would speak the last farewell, I cannot.
It would be still farewell a thousand times;
And, multiplied in echoes, still farewell.
I will not speak, but think a thousand thousand.
And be thou silent too, my last Sebastian;
So let us part in the dumb pomp of grief.
My heart's too great, or I would die this moment;
But death, I thank him, in an hour, has made
A mighty journey, and I haste to meet him.

[She staggers, and her **WOMEN** hold her up.

SEBASTIAN
Help to support this feeble drooping flower.
This tender sweet, so shaken by the storm;
For these fond arms must thus be stretched in vain,
And never, never must embrace her more.
'Tis past:—my soul goes in that word—farewell.

[**ALVAREZ** goes with **SEBASTIAN** to one end of the Stage; **WOMEN**, with **ALMEYDA,** to the other: **DORAX** coming up to **ANTONIO** and **MORAYMA**, who stand on the middle of the Stage.

DORAX
Haste to attend Almeyda:—For your sake
Your father is forgiven; but to Antonio
He forfeits half his wealth. Be happy both;
And let Sebastian and Almeyda's fate
This dreadful sentence to the world relate,—
That unrepented crimes, of parents dead,
Are justly punished on their children's head.

Footnotes:

1. This whimsical account of the Slave-market is probably taken from the following passage in the "Captivity and escape of Adam Elliot, M.A."—"By sun-rising next morning, we were all of us, who came last to Sallee, driven to market, where, the Moors sitting taylor-wise on stalls round about, we were severally run up and down by persons who proclaimed our qualities or trades, and what might best recommend us to the buyer. I had a great black who was appointed to sell me; this fellow, holding me by the hand, coursed me up and down from one person to another, who called upon me at pleasure to examine what trade I was of, and to see what labour my hands had been accustomed to. All the seamen were soon bought up, but it was mid-day ere I could meet with a purchaser."—See A modest Vindication of Titus Oates, London, 1682.

2. The knight much wondered at his sudden wit;
And said, The term of life is limited,
Ne may a man prolong nor shorten it;
The soldier may not move from watchful sted,
Nor leave his stand until his captain bed.
Fairy Queen, Book i. Canto 9.

3. The same artifice is used in "OEdipus," vol. vi. p. 149. To impress, by a description of the feelings of the unfortunate pair towards each other, a presentiment of their fatal relationship. The prophecy of Nostradamus is also obviously imitated from the response of the Delphic Pythoness to OEdipus.—Ibid. See p. 156.

4. For, interpreter; more usually spelled dragoman.

5. A horrid Moorish punishment. The criminal was precipitated from a high tower upon iron scythes and hooks, which projected from its side. This scene Settle introduces in one of his tragedies.

6. These presages of misfortune may remind the reader of the ominous feelings of the Duke of Guise, in the scene preceding his murder. The superstitious belief, that dejection of spirits, without cause, announces an impending violent death, is simply but well expressed in an old ballad called the "Warning to all Murderers:"

And after this most bad pretence,
The gentleman each day
Still felt his heart to throb and faint,
And sad he was alway.

His sleep was full of dreadful dreams,
In bed where he did lie;
His heart was heavy in the day,
Yet knew no reason why.

And oft as he did sit at meat,
His nose most suddenly
Would spring and gush out crimson blood,
And straight it would be dry.

7. There is great art in rendering the interpretation of this ominous dream so ingeniously doubtful. The latter circumstance, where the Emperor recognises his murderer as a personage in his vision, seems to be borrowed from the story of one of the caliphs, who, before his death, dreamed, that a sable hand and arm shook over his head a handful of red earth, and denounced, that such was the colour of the earth on which he should die. When taken ill on an expedition, he desired to know the colour of the earth on which his tent was pitched. A negro slave presented him with a specimen; and in the black's outstretched

arm, bared, from respect, to the elbow, as well as in the colour of the earth, the caliph acknowledged the apparition he had seen in his sleep, and prepared for immediate death.

8. Et quum fata volunt, bina venena juvant.—AUSONIUS.

9. Idiots were anciently wards of the crown; and the custody of their person, and charge of their estate, was often granted to the suit of some favourite, where the extent of the latter rendered it an object of plunder. Hence the common phrase of being begged for a fool.

10. This incident seems to be taken from the following passage in the Continuation of the Adventures of Don Sebastian.

"In Moran, an island some half league from Venice, there is an abbot called Capelo, a gentleman of Venice, a grave personage, and of great authority, hearing that the king laid wait for certain jewels that he had lost, (hoping thereby to recover some of them,) having a diamond in his keeping with the arms of Portugal, came to the town to the conventicles of St Francis, called Frari, where the king lay concealed, for that he was pursued by some that meant him no good, who no sooner beheld the ring, but he said, 'Verily this is mine, and I either lost the same in Flanders, or else it was stolen from me.' And when the king had put it upon his finger, it appeared otherwise engraven than before. The abbot enquiring of him that brought him the ring, how he came by it? he answered, it is true that the king hath said. Hence arose a strange rumour of a ring, that, by turning the stone, you might discern three great letters engraven, S.R.P. as much as to say, Sebastianus Rex Portugallix."—Harl. Mis. vol. v. p. 462.

11. It is said, in the pamphlets alluded to, that Don Sebastian, out of grief and shame for having fought against the advice of his generals, and lost the flower of his army, took the resolution of never returning to his country, but of burying himself in a hermitage; and that he resided for three years as an anchorite, on the top of a mountain in Dalmatia.

EPILOGUE,

SPOKEN BETWIXT ANTONIO AND MORAYMA

MORAYMA
I quaked at heart, for fear the royal fashion
Should have seduced us two to separation:
To be drawn in, against our own desire,
Poor I to be a nun, poor you, a friar.

ANTONIO
I trembled, when the old man's hand was in,
He would have proved we were too near of kin:
Discovering old intrigues of love, like t'other,
Betwixt my father and thy sinful mother;
To make us sister Turk and Christian brother.

MORAYMA
Excuse me there; that league should have been rather
Betwixt your mother and my Mufti father;
'Tis for my own and my relations' credit,
Your friends should bear the bastard, mine should get it.

ANTONIO
Suppose us two, Almeyda and Sebastian,
With incest proved upon us—

MORAYMA
Without question,
Their conscience was too queazy of digestion.

ANTONIO
Thou wouldst have kept the counsel of thy brother,
And sinned, till we repented of each other.

MORAYMA
Beast as you are, on Nature's laws to trample!
'Twere fitter that we followed their example.
And, since all marriage in repentance ends,
'Tis good for us to part when we are friends.
To save a maid's remorses and confusions,
E'en leave me now before we try conclusions.

ANTONIO
To copy their example, first make certain
Of one good hour, like theirs, before our parting;
Make a debauch, o'er night, of love and madness;
And marry, when we wake, in sober sadness.

MORAYMA
I'll follow no new sects of your inventing.
One night might cost me nine long months repenting;
First wed, and, if you find that life a fetter,
Die when you please; the sooner, sir, the better.
My wealth would get me love ere I could ask it:
Oh! there's a strange temptation in the casket.
All these young sharpers would my grace importune,
And make me thundering votes of lives and fortune[1].

Footnote

1. *Alluding to the addresses upon the Revolution.*

John Dryden – A Short Biography

John Dryden was born on August 9th, 1631 in the village rectory of Aldwincle near Thrapston in Northamptonshire, where his maternal grandfather was Rector of All Saints Church.

Dryden was the eldest of fourteen children born to Erasmus Dryden and wife Mary Pickering, paternal grandson of Sir Erasmus Dryden, 1st Baronet (1553–1632) and wife Frances Wilkes, Puritan landowning gentry who supported the Puritan cause and Parliament.

As a boy Dryden lived in the nearby village of Titchmarsh, Northamptonshire where it is probable that he received his first education.

In 1644 he was sent to Westminster School as a King's Scholar where his headmaster was Dr. Richard Busby, a charismatic teacher but severe disciplinarian. Having recently been re-founded by Elizabeth I, Westminster now embraced a very different religious and political spirit encouraging royalism and high Anglicanism but as a humanist public school, it maintained a curriculum which trained pupils in the art of rhetoric and the presentation of arguments for both sides of a given issue. This skill would remain with Dryden and influence his later writing and thinking, as much of it displays these dialectical patterns.

His first published poem, whilst still at Westminster, was an elegy with a strong royalist flavour on the death of his schoolmate Henry, Lord Hastings from smallpox, and alludes to the execution of King Charles I, which took place on January 30th, 1649.

In 1650 Dryden was ready for University and travelled to Trinity College, Cambridge. Dryden's undergraduate years would almost certainly have followed the standard curriculum of classics, rhetoric, and mathematics.

Dryden obtained his BA in 1654, graduating top of the list for Trinity that year.

However family tragedy struck in June of the same year when Dryden's father died, leaving him some land which generated a small income, but not enough to live on.

Returning to London during The Protectorate, Dryden now obtained work with Cromwell's Secretary of State, John Thurloe. This may have been the result of influence exercised on his behalf by his cousin the Lord Chamberlain, Sir Gilbert Pickering.

At Cromwell's funeral on 23 November 1658 Dryden was in the company of the Puritan poets John Milton and Andrew Marvell. The setting was to be a sea change in English history. From Republic to Monarchy and from one set of lauded poets to what would soon become the Age of Dryden.

The start began later that year when Dryden published the first of his great poems, Heroic Stanzas (1658), a eulogy on Cromwell's death which is necessarily cautious and prudent in its emotional display.

With the Restoration of the Monarchy in 1660 Dryden celebrated in verse with Astraea Redux, an authentic royalist panegyric. In this work the interregnum is illustrated as a time of anarchy, and Charles is seen as the restorer of peace and order.

With the king now established Dryden moved quickly to place himself as the leading poet and critic of his day and transferred his allegiances to the new government.

Along with Astraea Redux, Dryden welcomed the new regime with two more panegyrics: To His Sacred Majesty: A Panegyric on his Coronation (1662) and To My Lord Chancellor (1662).

These panegyrics are occasional and written to celebrate events. Thus they are written for the nation rather than the self, but these and others put him in good standing for his eventual appointment as Poet Laureate, where a number of event poems would be required each year and speaking for the Nation and to the Nation would be the first order of duty.

These poems suggest that Dryden was looking to court a possible patron which would have given him an income and time to explore his creative ideas but no, his path instead would be to make a living in writing for publishers, not for the aristocracy, and thus ultimately for the reading public.

In November 1662 Dryden was proposed for membership in the Royal Society, and he was elected an early fellow. However, his inactivity and non payment of dues led to his expulsion in 1666.

On December 1st, 1663 Dryden married the Royalist sister of Sir Robert Howard—Lady Elizabeth Howard (died 1714). The marriage was at St. Swithin's, London, and the consent of the parents is noted on the license, though Lady Elizabeth was then about twenty-five. She was the object of some scandals, well or ill founded; it was said that Dryden had been bullied into the marriage by her brothers. A small estate in Wiltshire was settled upon them by her father. The lady's intellect and temper were apparently not good; her husband was treated as an inferior by those of her social status.

Dryden's works occasionally contain outbursts against the married state but also celebrations of the same. Little else is known of the intimate side of his marriage.

Both Dryden and his wife were warmly attached to their children. They had three sons: Charles (1666–1704), John (1668–1701), and Erasmus Henry (1669–1710). Lady Elizabeth Dryden survived her husband, but went insane soon after his death and died in 1714.

With the re-opening of the theatres after the Puritan ban, Dryden began to also write plays. His first play, The Wild Gallant, appeared in 1663 but was not successful. From 1668 on he was contracted to produce three plays a year for the King's Company, in which he became a shareholder. During the 1660s and '70s, theatrical writing was his main source of income. He led the way in Restoration comedy, his best-known works being Marriage à la Mode (1672), as well as heroic tragedy and regular tragedy, in which his greatest success was All for Love (1678). Dryden was never fully satisfied with his theatrical writings and frequently suggested that his talents were wasted on unworthy audiences.

Certainly therefore fame as a poet looked more rewarding. In 1667, around the same time his dramatic career began, he published Annus Mirabilis, a lengthy historical poem which described the English defeat of the Dutch naval fleet and the Great Fire of London in 1666. It was a modern epic in pentameter quatrains that established him as the pre-eminent poet of his generation, and was crucial in his attaining the posts of Poet Laureate (1668) and then historiographer royal (1670).

When the Great Plague of London closed the theatres in 1665 Dryden retreated to Wiltshire where he wrote Of Dramatick Poesie (1668), arguably the best of his unsystematic prefaces and essays. Dryden constantly defended his own literary practice, and Of Dramatick Poesie, the longest of his critical works, takes the form of a dialogue in which four characters—each based on a prominent contemporary, with Dryden himself as 'Neander'—debate the merits of classical, French and English drama.

He felt strongly about the relation of the poet to tradition and the creative process, and his heroic play Aureng-zebe (1675) has a prologue which denounces the use of rhyme in serious drama. His play All for Love (1678) was written in blank verse, and was to immediately follow Aureng-Zebe.

On December 18th, 1679 he was attacked in Rose Alley near his home in Covent Garden by thugs hired by fellow poet, John Wilmot, 2nd Earl of Rochester, with whom he had a long-standing conflict. Wilmot was constantly in and out of favour with the King and his own poetry was often bawdy, lewd, even obscene and made fun of the King who would often exile him from Court.

Dryden's greatest achievements were in satiric verse: the mock-heroic Mac Flecknoe, a more personal product of his Laureate years, was a lampoon circulated in manuscript and an attack on the playwright Thomas Shadwell. Dryden's main goal in the work is to "satirize Shadwell, ostensibly for his offenses against literature but more immediately we may suppose for his habitual badgering of him on the stage and in print." It is not a belittling form of satire, but rather one which makes its object great in ways which are unexpected, transferring the ridiculous into poetry. This line of satire continued with Absalom and Achitophel (1681) and The Medal (1682). Other major works from this period are the religious poems Religio Laici (1682), written from the position of a member of the Church of England; his 1683 edition of Plutarch's Lives, translated From the Greek by Several Hands in which he introduced the word biography to English readers; and The Hind and the Panther, (1687) which celebrates his conversion to Roman Catholicism.

He wrote Britannia Rediviva celebrating the birth of a son and heir to the Catholic King and Queen on June 10th, 1688. When later in the same year James II was deposed in the Glorious Revolution, Dryden's refusal to take the oaths of allegiance to the new monarchs, William and Mary, which left him out of favour at court and he had to leave his post as Poet Laureate. Thomas Shadwell, his despised rival, succeeded him. Dryden, England's greatest literary figure, was now forced to give up his public offices and live by the proceeds of his pen alone.

Dryden was an excellent translator with his own style which brought the ire of many critics. Many felt he would embellish or expand anything he felt short or curt. Dryden did not feel such expansion was a fault, arguing that as Latin is a naturally concise language it cannot be duly represented by a comparable number of words in the much larger English vocabulary. He continued with his task of translating works by Horace, Juvenal, Ovid, Lucretius, and Theocritus, a task which he found far more satisfying than writing for the stage.

In 1694 he began work on what would be his most ambitious and defining work as translator, The Works of Virgil (1697), which was published by subscription. The publication of the translation of Virgil was a national event and brought Dryden the sum of £1,400.

His final translations appeared in the volume Fables Ancient and Modern (1700), a series of episodes from Homer, Ovid, and Boccaccio, as well as modernised adaptations from Geoffrey Chaucer interspersed with Dryden's own poems. As a translator, he made great literary works in the older languages available to readers of English.

John Dryden died on May 12th, 1700, and was initially buried in St. Anne's cemetery in Soho, before being exhumed and reburied in Westminster Abbey ten days later. He was the subject of poetic eulogies, such as Luctus Brittannici: or the Tears of the British Muses; for the Death of John Dryden, Esq. (London, 1700), and The Nine Muses.

He is seen as dominating the literary life of Restoration England to such a point that the period came to be known in literary circles as the Age of Dryden. Walter Scott called him "Glorious John."

Dryden was the dominant literary figure and influence of his age. He established the heroic couplet as a standard form of English poetry by writing successful satires, religious pieces, fables, epigrams, compliments, prologues, and plays with it; he also introduced the alexandrine and triplet into the form. In his poems, translations, and criticism, he established a poetic diction appropriate to the heroic couplet—Auden referred to him as "the master of the middle style"—that was a model for his contemporaries and for much of the 18th century. The considerable loss felt by the English literary community at his death was evident in the elegies written about him. Dryden's heroic couplet went on to become the dominant poetic form of the 18th century.

What Dryden achieved in his poetry was neither the emotional excitement of the early nineteenth-century romantics nor the intellectual complexities of the metaphysicals. Although he uses formal structures such as heroic couplets, he tried to recreate the natural rhythm of speech, and he knew that different subjects need different kinds of verse. In his preface to Religio Laici he says that "the expressions of a poem designed purely for instruction ought to be plain and natural, yet majestic... The florid, elevated and figurative way is for the passions; for (these) are begotten in the soul by showing the objects out of their true proportion.... A man is to be cheated into passion, but to be reasoned into truth."

Perhaps the following illustrates Dryden and his life—"The way I have taken, is not so streight as Metaphrase, nor so loose as Paraphrase: Some things too I have omitted, and sometimes added of my own. Yet the omissions I hope, are but of Circumstances, and such as wou'd have no grace in English; and the Addition, I also hope, are easily deduc'd from Virgil's Sense. They will seem (at least I have the Vanity to think so), not struck into him, but growing out of him".

John Dryden – A Concise Bibliography

Astraea Redux, 1660
The Wild Gallant (comedy), 1663
The Indian Emperour (tragedy), 1665
Annus Mirabilis (poem), 1667
The Enchanted Island (comedy), 1667, with William D'Avenant from Shakespeare's The Tempest
Secret Love, or The Maiden Queen, 1667
An Essay of Dramatick Poesie, 1668
An Evening's Love (comedy), 1668
Tyrannick Love (tragedy), 1669
The Conquest of Granada, 1670
The Assignation, or Love in a Nunnery, 1672
Marriage à la mode, 1672

Amboyna, or the Cruelties of the Dutch to the English Merchants, 1673
The Mistaken Husband (comedy), 1674
Aureng-zebe, 1675
All for Love, 1678
Oedipus (heroic drama), 1679, an adaptation with Nathaniel Lee of Sophocles' Oedipus
Absalom and Achitophel, 1681
The Spanish Fryar, 1681
Mac Flecknoe, 1682
The Medal, 1682
Religio Laici, 1682
To the Memory of Mr. Oldham, 1684
Threnodia Augustalis, 1685
The Hind and the Panther, 1687
A Song for St. Cecilia's Day, 1687
Britannia Rediviva, 1688, written to mark the birth of a Prince of Wales.
Amphitryon, 1690
Don Sebastian (play), 1690
Creator Spirit, by whose aid, 1690. Translation of Rabanus Maurus' Veni Creator Spiritus
King Arthur, 1691
Cleomenes, 1692
The Art of Satire, 1693
Love Triumphant, 1694
The Works of Virgil, 1697
Alexander's Feast, 1697
Fables, Ancient and Modern, 1700

www.ingramcontent.com/pod-product-compliance
Lightning Source LLC
Chambersburg PA
CBHW061947070426
42450CB00007BA/1083